Recipes

for the

Good Life

11/08

Recipes

for the

Good Life

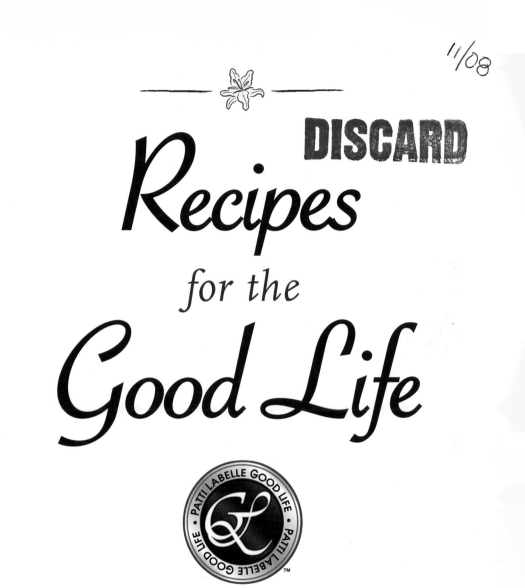

PATTI LaBELLE

with JUDITH CHOATE AND KAREN HUNTER

Karen Hunter Publishing,
A Division of Suitt-Hunter Enterprises, LLC
598 Broadway, 3rd Floor
New York, NY 10012

First Karen Hunter Publishing hardcover edition November 2008

For information about special discounts for bulk purchases, please contact
Simon & Schuster Special Sales at 1-800-456-6798 or business@simonandschuster.com.

LAYOUT AND DESIGN: Joel Avirom and Jason Snyder
JACKET DESIGN: Stephanie DeBoer and Andrew Fuhrmann
RECIPE TESTING: James Canora
COPYEDITING: Sara Newberry and David Kokakis
CULINARY CONSULTING: Sonia Armstead and Rochelle Brown
PHOTOGRAPHY: Steven Freeman
FOOD STYLIST: Duana Maxwell
ASSISTANT FOOD STYLIST: Dave Martin
EXECUTIVE PRODUCTION: Zuri Edwards, Elan Kaufman, Charles Suitt,
David Kokakis, and Andrew Fuhrmann

Manufactured in the United States of America

1   3   5   7   9   10   8   6   4   2

ISBN-13: 978-1-4391-0152-0
ISBN-10:   1-4391-0152-3

To all my fans.

It is your love that has kept me going all of these years and this book is my way of giving some of that love back. Every recipe in this book was made with love—it is the most important ingredient.

Many people can throw a meal together, but those who cook with love have more than a meal—they have the makings of a good life!

Thank you and may God bless each and every one of you!

Contents

Introduction: The Good Life 9

Miss Patti's Perfect Pantry 14

Setting the Right Mood for the Food 19

Hot 'n' Spicy (Like Me!) 23

Down-Home Stick to Your Ribs Meals 49

Light & Healthy
(But It Still Tastes Great!) 79

Smack Yo' Mama Seafood 105

Celebrate! Bangin' Barbecues,
Beautiful Brunches, and Happy Holidays 135

Cakes, Pies, and Other Things
I Shouldn't Eat 193

List of Recipes and Index 219

The Good Life

Over the years I've talked about how devastating it was to lose all of my sisters to cancer and all before the age of forty-four. But what I haven't talked much about was how I decided to live my life after they died. I was certain that I was going to be the next to go, so I started "living to die." It was like I was on Death Row, and instead of living each day to the fullest, I was just going through the motions of life. I stopped caring, because, after all, I would be dead soon, right?

Well, age forty-four passed me right by and I was still around. Then I hit that magic number—fifty—and I thought, "Why am I still here?" When I finally figured out that God wasn't ready for me yet, I made up my mind that I would stop living to die and start really living to live! By the time I reached age sixty, I was living out loud, living each day to the fullest, living my best life—living the good life!

To me, living the good life means many things. It means living a healthy lifestyle and taking care of the body I have by exercising and eating right (most of the time!). It means surrounding myself with good people with good energy and getting rid of anyone and anything that might be a drag. I sometimes find myself telling people, in a nice way, of course, "Who do I look like, a professional therapist? You better get away from me with your problems!" Living the good life means enjoying each day—whether it's sunny or rainy—and finding the joy in it. Living the good life means treating myself like a queen.

You don't need a whole bunch of money to live your good life. I've had money and still didn't take care of myself the way I should have. I would work and work and work and not get enough sleep, not drink enough water, not exercise at all and let people drain me with their negativity. I didn't pay attention to the little things. I was both rich and broke at the same time. So, living the good life is not about having lots of money (don't get me wrong, it's more fun *with* money). Instead, living the good life is simply about putting yourself first. It's about doing things for yourself and making *you* a priority in your own life. Many of us spend so much time taking care of others and making sure those we love are happy, but you can't help someone else until you take care of yourself first. And it's tough to show everyone else love unless you love yourself first.

It starts with the little things—taking a warm bath once a week, pampering yourself, getting a pedicure or finding a fragrance that makes you feel good. I never realized how much the little things mattered—something as simple as your bedding can make a big difference in your life. I used to sleep on anything. I didn't care if my sheets came from the dollar store. I didn't think it mattered. Then, about twenty years ago when I was living in Los Angeles, I stopped into this cute store that sold things for the house. They had these cotton sheets with a high thread count—I didn't even know what a "thread count" was back then. But when I slept on them for the first time, I felt like I was sleeping on silk clouds. It was the best night's sleep I had ever had, and I refuse to go back to cheap sheets now. But it's really not about the sheets

or about them being more expensive than the sheets I used to sleep on—it's about giving myself the best, because I deserve it.

I have a guest bathroom in my house that is filled with pictures, a couple of my gold records, a letter from a former president of the United States, and beautiful trinkets and flowers. All of the fixtures are elaborate and over the top, just the way I like it. It's so fierce that people walk through it as one of the entrances in my house and don't even notice that it is a bathroom. But it *is* a bathroom—Miss Patti style. I want people to feel as wonderful as I do, no matter what room of the house they're in.

My entire home is dedicated to celebrating the good life. There are photos of me everywhere because I *love* me. But what I love just as much are the photos of people who have touched my life—some who aren't with me anymore, such as my parents, my sisters and brother, my friend Luther Vandross, and my dear musical director, Bud Ellison. Those photos make me feel like they are right there in the room with me and it brings me joy to look at those smiling faces and remember the good times we had together. A lot of my memories with my loved ones are set around a dinner table, sharing a meal and sharing good conversation. Food has always been at the center of my joy, from the fish fries my parents had every weekend to the barbecues I have in my backyard today. Food can bring people together, to laugh, to eat, and to simply celebrate life. Most people know me for my voice, and that is truly a gift from God. But food and the ability to share it with others is also a gift—a gift that you can give to those you love. It is with that spirit that I share my third cookbook.

My first cookbook, *LaBelle Cuisine: Recipes to Sing About,* was filled with recipes that I loved, but those meals could sure clog some arteries with all the eggs, cheeses, and butter. I love that food and it makes me happy, but I can't eat that way today—at least not every day. My second book, *Patti LaBelle Lite Cuisine,* was my way of enjoying some of those same foods from the first book with a few modifications. I had to find a way to make meals that fit into my new lifestyle as a diabetic. Although I had diabetes, I was not going to let diabetes have me. I was going to live my life and enjoy my food, but I had to do it another way.

In this cookbook there are some recipes like the ones in my first cookbook, because that's some good food! But there are also plenty of healthy choices, like the ones in my second cookbook. This book is about living a balanced life. It is a celebration of life. If I want some chocolate, I don't deprive myself. If I want some of the fried apple pie that's in this book, I will have a slice. Everything in moderation. It's about being fierce, being balanced, and being happy. Living your good life is about having it *all*!

You'll see throughout the book that I have used products from my Patti LaBelle Good Life product line. The philosophy behind the brand is that the good life can be enjoyed by everyone, regardless of background or how much money you have. It's not about spending a lot of money—it's about making what you do spend count, taking pride in what you have, and pampering yourself in little ways that make you feel special. This is the thinking behind my signature line of products—it's accessible to everyone, reasonably priced, simple, and from my heart. So, here's perhaps the most important recipe in this entire book, so memorize it—it's my recipe for living the good life: keep it simple, make it special, share your heart, and pamper yourself!

Miss Patti's Perfect Pantry

"**S**tay ready, so you don't have to get ready." Be prepared! I never want to be caught off guard—whether it's on stage or in my kitchen. If some friends drop by unannounced, I'm always ready for them because I stay ready. There is no running to the store at the last minute to pick up a few things. I always have something in my refrigerator or pantry that can be made into a spread at a moment's notice.

I would like to share with you a few things that you should always have in your fridge, freezer and pantry—so on any given day, or any time of day, if you want to get down to business in the kitchen you will have the basics and you will be prepared.

Here are the must-haves:

SPICES

Sea salt	Paprika
Kosher salt	Cayenne pepper
Black pepper	Cinnamon (ground)
Seasoned salt	Nutmeg (ground)
Garlic powder	Vanilla extract
Onion powder	Cloves
Italian seasoning	Crushed red pepper flakes

CANNED GOODS

Chicken broth	Tomato paste
Beef broth	Marinara sauce
Vegetable broth	Canned beans (black and white beans)
Canned tomatoes (crushed, plum and whole)	Tuna
Tomato sauce	Salmon

FREEZER ITEMS

Frozen vegetables	Ground beef
Chicken parts	Ground turkey
Chicken breast	

REFRIGERATOR ITEMS

Milk	Ginger root
Eggs	Olives
Butter	Mustard
Cheese (cheddar and parmesan)	Ketchup
Onions	Mayonnaise
Peppers	Soy sauce
Carrots	Salsa
Lemons	Balsamic vinegar
Limes	

Sugar

Brown sugar

Sugar substitute

Flour

Cornstarch

Vegetable oil

Extra-virgin olive oil

Spaghetti

Penne or bow-tie pasta

Egg noodles

White rice

Brown rice

Crackers

Breadcrumbs

And last, but certainly not least, try to keep a full stock of my Patti LaBelle Good Life products! Here are some of the ones that can make your time in the kitchen a bit easier:

PATTI LABELLE PREMIUM ALL NATURAL PEPPER PRODUCTS

LaBelle Diced Fine Jalapeños

LaBelle Sweet Hot Jalapeño Relish

LaBelle Rich Red Hot Sauce

LaBelle Hot Flash Hot Sauce

LaBelle Pepper Clear Mild Pepper Sauce

PATTI LABELLE "JUST PLAIN GOOD" BLENDED SEASONINGS

Seasoned Sea Salt

Seasoned Pepper

Chili & Dill Sea Salt

Garlic Pepper Seasoning

Miss Patti's No Salt Seasoning

For more information about the Patti LaBelle Good Life product line, visit WWW.PATTILABELLEFOODS.COM

PATTI LABELLE PREMIUM ALL NATURAL PEPPER PRODUCTS

PATTI LABELLE "JUST PLAIN GOOD" BLENDED SEASONINGS

Setting the Right Mood for the Food

$\mathcal{F}$ood is the focus of this book, but don't forget that what happens in the kitchen is only part of making a good meal. Other things, such as setting the table properly, playing the right music, seating guests in a way that makes sense, and creating a pleasing atmosphere, are all important ingredients in my recipe for a perfect occasion.

I love to entertain, but I don't just jump into a party without preparation. I know things around my home seem thrown together, but I actually have a plan. If the plates don't match, I planned it that way. If it's a buffet-style meal instead of a sit-down dinner, that wasn't by accident, either. Whether it's a dinner party, a Christmas party, or just a family or friend get-together, I have a plan. It starts with the table—which is center stage. I make sure I have my china and stemware out. Now don't worry if you have a bunch of pieces that don't match up, because many of my china and stemware items don't match. But I pull it all together, Patti-style. How? With color. I will pick a particular color scheme (I love bold, bright, cheery colors) and I make sure that the accents are in perfect harmony. I will decorate the table with flowers and candles (unscented, please, because you don't want to take away from the aroma of the good food you worked so hard to prepare). Candles and flowers on a table make everything pop. Sometimes I'll set a table and not even allow people to eat on it! I want that table to be the star. I don't want anyone spilling gravy or red wine on the tablecloth or messing up the look.

Once you've set the proper mood, now you want to make sure you get people mingling. Don't just usher guests to the table as soon as they walk in the door. Leave ample time before the meal to allow people to chat informally. Encourage them to move around. If you really want to get people talking to each other at the next party you host, try this: send out invitations with a little note inside, or pass the notes out to each person upon arrival at the party—each note will have a one-sentence description of a different guest at the party—it's each person's responsibility to mingle around, asking questions of each other, trying to identify the guest who is described on his or her personal note. This type of getting-to-know-you game is a lot of fun. Feel free to make up your own. Get creative!

During a meal guests have to sit next to each other for at least the first few courses. So, I make sure the seating chart makes sense. Yes, I assign seats to ensure that everyone mixes and mingles. I've found that people leave my parties much richer because they have forged new friendships.

Personal touches are very important. For instance, if you're having a get-together for your girlfriends, find out each lady's favorite flower and color, and that becomes their personal place setting at the table. It's a great way to add flowers to the table and get away from the typical centerpiece. It also makes each guest feel special. Make sure you put a vase in the center of the table so that each guest can put her flower in there, so that it's out of the way when the meal is served. You can also see how creative the arrangement becomes with all of the wonderful, different flowers coming together. From all of the individual floral settings, you will now have one beautiful centerpiece that everyone created together.

And don't forget the music! Music can make or break the mood, so put some careful thought into this. If it's an intimate brunch, keep the music mellow and low in the background. If it's a lively gathering, select music that's a bit more up-tempo and kick the volume up a notch. For those backyard cookouts, invite your guests to bring their favorite CDs so they feel like they're contributing to the event—and turn the volume up, up, up! And try not to rely on playing the radio, because it can be a little annoying when the music is interrupted by commercials. Instead, pull out your CDs, records, or 8-track tapes (if you go that far back!) and put something together that's special. You don't need to be a professional DJ to make it work—just go with what feels right.

Hot 'n' Spicy (Like Me!)

My favorite foods typically incorporate hot sauce in some way, shape or form. Not only do I love the flavor, but research has shown that hot sauce and peppers not only burn your mouth, they also burn calories and speed up your metabolism—so it's not just good, it's good for you! Now, I'm no doctor and I'm not saying that hot sauce is a magical, cure-all potion, but I do know I love the way it makes me feel when I use it to spice up my food.

The first time I ever tasted hot, spicy food, I had to be about eight years old. I ate a piece of fried chicken with hot sauce off of my daddy's plate. It had me running for a glass of water. My mouth was on fire! "Girl, I don't know how you could eat that," my mother said to me, laughing and shaking her head.

My father didn't just love his food spicy, he loved it *hot*. I mean, hot-hot! I learned to appreciate my father's love for hot food. The more I ate it, the more I got to enjoy the flavor after the fire died down. I got so into spicy foods that I used to experiment, making my own "hot sauce." I would take some ketchup out of the refrigerator and put it in a bowl. I would then chop up some jalapeno, habanero or any kind of hot pepper my mother had around, and I would mix it with the ketchup. Finally, to add insult to injury, I would stir in some black pepper. My parents must have loved me, because they actually tried this concoction and told me it was good.

Today, I rarely eat anything without sprinkling a little (or a lot, depending what it is) of hot sauce on my food. I'm even known for traveling with a bottle of hot sauce in my purse. I never know when a restaurant or hotel will serve bland food, so I have to be prepared!

This is one of my favorite chapters in this book because it is a celebration of a flavor that reminds me of my daddy and reminds me of my discovery of real flavors. I love spices so much that I had to create my own line of pepper products. My favorite to carry around is called "Hot Flash" and it's all that and then some. It's the perfect blend of habanero and jalapeño peppers—and somewhat resembles the recipe I came up with as a child, but it tastes a whole lot better! It has just the right amount of fire. There are other sauces in my line of products for those who can't take it really hot. Most people really love the "Rich Red," named after my dear friend, Denise Rich. It's slammin' when used on some fried fish or chicken wings. Hot sauces really do add something special to the dishes.

ZURI'S HOT LIKE THAT BUFFALO WINGS

LABELLE SPICED-UP BEEF TIPS

SLOPPY JOES À LA PATTI

MY FAVORITE SPICED BEEF RIBS

SASSY CHICKEN PARMESAN

MAMA'S OLE TIME SHRIMP CREOLE

LABELLE SEAFOOD SALAD

SPICY DIRTY RICE

MISS PATTI'S CABBAGE SHUFFLE

VIDALIA ONION BLOSSOM

OOH-LA-LABELLE TURKEY CHILI

MISS PATTI'S HOT CHEESE BISCUITS

2½ to 3 pounds chicken wings, tips
    removed

¼ cup butter, melted

6 tablespoons LaBelle Rich Red Hot
    Sauce

1 teaspoon paprika

1 teaspoon LaBelle Seasoned Sea Salt

½ teaspoon cayenne pepper

¼ teaspoon ground black pepper

Blue Cheese Dip (recipe follows)

I think that my son Zuri could eat this entire mess of wings all by his lonesome. My Rich Red Hot Sauce is his favorite, so I incorporated it in this recipe. But it's also spiced up with cayenne and black pepper. I guess Zuri is following in his grandpa's shoes!

SERVES 4 TO 6

ZURI'S HOT LIKE THAT BUFFALO WINGS

1. Using a sharp knife, cut each wing into 2 pieces, the drumette and the second joint. Rinse under cold, running water and pat dry. Place the wings in a large resealable plastic bag.

2. Combine the melted butter with the Rich Red sauce, paprika, seasoning salt, cayenne, and black pepper. Reserving 2 tablespoons on the side, pour the marinade into the plastic bag. Seal and push the wings around to ensure an even coating. Set aside to marinate for 30 minutes.

3. Preheat the broiler.

4. Remove the chicken wings from the plastic bag, discarding the leftover marinade.

5. Place the wings on a broiler pan in a single layer. Place under the preheated broiler, about 5 inches from the flame. Broil, turning once or twice, for 18 minutes or until the chicken is thoroughly cooked and nicely charred. Watch carefully, because you don't want the wings to burn!

6. Remove the wings from the broiler and place on a serving platter. Pour the reserved 2 tablespoons of marinade over the top and toss to coat.

7. Serve with Blue Cheese Dip along with carrot and celery sticks, if desired.

BLUE CHEESE DIP

1. Combine the cheese and milk in a small bowl. Using a fork, mash the mixture together until creamy, with very few lumps. Stir in the mayonnaise, sour cream, and lemon juice. When well blended, stir in the garlic and season with pepper to taste.

2. Cover and refrigerate for 30 minutes before serving to allow the flavors to blend.

3 ounces blue cheese, crumbled

¼ cup milk

½ cup mayonnaise

½ cup sour cream

1 tablespoon fresh lemon juice

1 clove garlic, peeled and minced

Ground black pepper to taste

2 pounds beef tips

1 tablespoon Worcestershire sauce

Salt and freshly ground pepper to taste

2 tablespoons "lite" olive oil

1 medium onion, peeled and sliced

1 green bell pepper, well-washed, cored,
    seeded, membrane removed, and sliced

1 cup sliced mushrooms

3 tablespoons LaBelle Diced Fine Jalapeños

1 cup low-sodium beef broth

6 cups cooked rice

*I*f you keep a jar of LaBelle Diced Fine Jalapeños handy, you can easily spice up your table. With nothing more than jalapeños and a little vinegar as a preservative, these little pieces of heat will light up any recipe.

SERVES 6

LaBelle Spiced-Up Beef Tips

1. Season the beef tips with Worcestershire sauce and salt and pepper to taste.

2. Heat the oil in a large nonstick frying pan over medium-high heat. When very hot, but not smoking, add the beef. Cook, stirring occasionally, for about 3 minutes or until the beef is nicely browned. Remove the beef from the pan and set aside.

3. Add the onion, bell pepper, mushrooms and jalapeños to the pan, stirring to combine. Add the broth, stirring to release any browned bits from the bottom of the pan. Cover and bring to a simmer. Lower the heat and simmer for about 15 minutes or until the broth has reduced by half.

4. Return the beef tips to the pan and bring to a simmer. Simmer for 10 minutes or until the beef is tender.

5. Remove from the heat, taste, and, if necessary, season with salt and pepper. Serve over hot rice.

*K*ids, grown-ups, old folks—everyone loves my Sloppy Joes. These are quick to put together when the guys are watching a game or when we girls are gathered for some gossip and fun. If you don't have my products on hand, make the mix using fresh jalapeños and sweet pickle relish with some hot sauce added.

SERVES 6

2 pounds ground turkey

1 cup minced red onion

½ cup diced green bell pepper

1 tablespoon minced garlic

1 teaspoon chili powder

½ teaspoon seasoned salt

2 cups tomato sauce

2 tablespoons LaBelle Diced Fine Jalapeños

6 large slices Italian bread, toasted or seeded rolls, split

6 tablespoons LaBelle Sweet Hot Jalapeño Relish

SLOPPY JOES À LA PATTI

1. Place the turkey, onion, bell pepper, and garlic in a nonstick frying pan over medium heat. Season with the chili powder and salt. Fry, stirring frequently to break up the meat, for about 10 minutes or until the meat has browned. Stir in the tomato sauce and jalapeños and continue to cook for another 10 minutes.

2. Remove from the heat and serve, open-face, on toasted Italian bread or seeded rolls, topped with the relish.

6 pounds beef spareribs, cut into ribs

½ cup LaBelle Hot Flash Hot Sauce

2 tablespoons light brown sugar

2 tablespoons ground black pepper

2 tablespoons chili powder

2 tablespoons paprika

2 teaspoons salt

2 teaspoons dried parsley flakes

1 teaspoon onion powder

1 teaspoon crushed red pepper flakes

1 cup barbecue sauce (use your favorite bottled brand)

*M*eaty beef ribs can be spiced-up better than anything I know. Marinating the beef overnight causes the pepper mix to really penetrate the meat so there's no denying that you've got some spice in your life. If you want to use these for a main course, just double the recipe.

SERVES 6

MY FAVORITE SPICED BEEF RIBS

1. Bring a large pot of cold, salted water to a boil over high heat. Add the ribs and return to a boil. Lower the heat and simmer for 30 minutes. Remove from the heat and drain well. Set aside to cool. When cool, pat very dry with paper towel.

2. Combine the hot sauce with the brown sugar, pepper, chili powder, paprika, salt, parsley flakes, onion powder, and crushed red pepper flakes.

3. Put on gloves and rub the spice blend into the dry ribs. Place the seasoned ribs in a large pan, cover tightly with aluminum foil, and refrigerate overnight (or for at least 8 hours).

4. About 30 minutes before you're ready to grill, remove the ribs from the refrigerator so that they can come to room temperature.

5. Oil and preheat the grill to medium.

6. Place the ribs in a single layer on the grill. Grill, turning often, for 20 minutes. Brush with a light coating of barbecue sauce and continue to grill, turning often, for 10 more minutes or until nicely charred and tender.

6 boneless, skinless chicken breast halves

1 tablespoon crushed red pepper flakes, or to taste

1 teaspoon garlic powder

Salt and ground black pepper to taste

2 large eggs

¼ cup milk

2 tablespoons grated Parmesan cheese

1 cup Italian-seasoned breadcrumbs

½ cup "lite" olive oil

One 32-ounce jar spaghetti sauce, choose your favorite—this gives enough to serve on a side of spaghetti—cook the pasta while the chicken is baking

¼ cup LaBelle Rich Red Hot Sauce

1 cup shredded mozzarella cheese

*Y*ou get your heat from two directions in my special Chicken Parmesan—in the chicken and in the sauce. I buy a big jar of sauce so I have enough left to serve with spaghetti (be sure to doctor it up with Hot Flash). I add a great green salad and some of my spicy garlic bread. You can just call me Mama Patrizia!

SERVES 6

SASSY CHICKEN PARMESAN

1. Preheat the oven to 375°F.

2. Season the chicken with pepper flakes and garlic powder along with salt and pepper to taste, pressing the seasoning into the flesh.

3. Combine the eggs with the milk and Parmesan cheese in a shallow bowl, beating with a fork to combine.

4. Place the breadcrumbs in another shallow bowl.

5. Working with one piece at a time, dip the chicken breasts into the egg mixture and then into the breadcrumbs, pushing down to completely coat each side with breading.

6. Heat the oil in a large frying pan over medium-high heat. When very hot, but not smoking, add the breaded chicken breasts. Fry, turning once (very carefully so you don't break the breading), for about 6 minutes or until golden brown and partially cooked.

7. Transfer the fried chicken to a double layer of paper towel to drain off excess oil.

8. When well-drained, place the chicken in a single layer in an 11-inch rectangular baking dish.

9. Combine 1¼ cups of the spaghetti sauce with the Hot Flash and pour 3 tablespoons of the sauce over each chicken breast. Tightly enclose the whole pan with aluminum foil. Place in the preheated oven and bake for 15 minutes.

10. Uncover and discard the foil. Sprinkle the top with the mozzarella cheese and continue to bake for another 5 minutes or until the cheese has melted and taken on a bit of color.

11. Remove from the oven and serve with a side of spaghetti, if desired.

3 tablespoons canola oil

10 cloves garlic, peeled and minced

1 cup diced onions

½ cup diced celery

½ cup diced green bell pepper

3 tablespoons all-purpose flour

2½ cups canned diced tomatoes with their juice

1 tablespoon white vinegar

½ cup water

1 bay leaf

1 tablespoon LaBelle Diced Fine Jalapeños

1½ teaspoon dried thyme

1 teaspoon chili powder

½ teaspoon dried oregano

1 tablespoon LaBelle Hot Flash Hot Sauce

Salt and pepper to taste

3 pounds medium shrimp, peeled and deveined

1 cup thawed frozen peas

8 cups hot cooked rice—white or brown

2 tablespoons chopped parsley

There's nothing like a pot of Big Easy Creole. This recipe can easily be doubled or tripled for when you need to feed a crowd. Just have lots of rice and plenty of sweet tea or beer to soothe the heat!

SERVES 6 TO 8

MAMA'S OLE TIME SHRIMP CREOLE

1. Heat the oil in a large heavy bottomed saucepan over medium heat. When hot, stir in the garlic, onions, celery, bell pepper and cook, stirring frequently, for 5 minutes or until the vegetables have softened slightly and begun to color. Stir in the flour, lower the heat and cook, stirring constantly, for about 10 minutes or until the mixture has turned a deep golden brown. Stir in the tomatoes and vinegar along with a ½ cup of water. Raise the heat and bring to a boil. Stir in the bay leaf, jalapeños, thyme, chili powder, and oregano. When blended, stir in the hot sauce and let cook for 1 minute.

2. Season with salt and pepper to taste, immediately lower the heat, and cook at a gentle simmer for 20 minutes or until the flavors are well-blended and the sauce has thickened.

3. Stir in the shrimp and peas and cook for about 5 minutes or just until the shrimp have cooked through. Remove from the heat.

4. Mound the rice on a serving platter. Spoon the creole over the top, sprinkle with parsley, and serve with more Hot Flash on the side.

1 pound lump crabmeat, picked clean
of all shell and cartilage

½ pound cooked shrimp, peeled,
deveined, and chopped

2 tablespoons minced onion

2 tablespoon finely diced red bell pepper

½ cup mayonnaise

2 tablespoons LaBelle Sweet Hot
Jalapeño Relish

1 tablespoon LaBelle Hot Flash
Hot Sauce

½ teaspoon dry mustard powder

Juice of ½ lemon

Salt to taste

6 large cooked tails-on shrimp, peeled
and deveined

6 parsley sprigs

LaBelle Pepper Clear Mild Pepper
Sauce for drizzling

*W*hy "La Belle" Seafood Salad? Because it's such a beautiful salad, that's why. And since it's my invention, it makes a great play on my name. I have always loved the seafood salads served in Italian restaurants and decided it was time to make one at home. Those few little red pepper flakes in the classic salad get booted for a mix of my hot sauces and relish. And, served in a martini glass, it is a pretty classy first course!

SERVES 6

LaBelle Seafood Salad

1. Combine the crabmeat, shrimp, onion and bell pepper in a mixing bowl. Set aside.

2. Combine the mayonnaise with the relish, Hot Flash and mustard powder in a small mixing bowl. When blended, add the lemon juice and salt to taste.

3. Pour the mayonnaise mixture over the crabmeat mixture, gently stirring to just combine—be careful not to break up all of the crabmeat.

4. Place an equal portion of the salad in each of 6 martini glasses. Place a whole shrimp and a sprig of parsley on top of each one. Drizzle with Pepper Clear and serve.

2 tablespoons canola oil

5 cloves garlic, peeled and minced

1 medium onion, peeled and chopped

½ cup chopped celery

½ cup chopped green bell pepper

1 pound ground turkey

1 pound Italian-style hot turkey
    sausage, removed from the casing

2 tablespoons LaBelle Diced Fine
    Jalapeños

Salt and pepper to taste

1 cup raw long-grain white rice

2½ cups hot low-sodium chicken broth

2 teaspoons LaBelle Seasoned Pepper
    Blend or your favorite LaBelle
    blended seasoning to taste

½ cup chopped scallions

Dirty Rice isn't dirty at all, but a great Cajun dish made with chicken giblets. Its name comes from the dark color that the chopped liver gives to the cooked rice. Eating Cajun food can get pretty down and dirty though, as the Cajuns love their spice about as much as I do! My recipe is pretty meaty with lots of turkey and turkey sausage, so it could easily be served as a main course rather than a side.

SERVES 6

SPICY DIRTY RICE

1. Heat the oil in a large nonstick frying pan over medium heat. Add the garlic, onion, celery, and bell pepper, stirring to blend. Cook, stirring frequently, for about 3 minutes or until the vegetables have wilted and the garlic is golden. Add the turkey and turkey sausage, and cook, stirring to break up the meat, for about 7 minutes or until nicely browned. Add the jalapeños and season with salt and pepper.

2. Stir in the rice. Add the broth and blackened spice and bring to a boil.

3. Lower the heat, cover, and simmer for about 25 minutes or until the rice is tender.

4. Remove from the heat. Stir in the scallions. Taste and, if necessary, add salt and pepper and serve.

2 tablespoons "lite" olive oil

2 russet potatoes, peeled and cut into
    1-inch cubes

2 medium carrots, peeled, trimmed
    and cut, crosswise, into thick slices

1 medium onion, peeled and sliced

1 large red bell pepper, well-washed,
    cored, seeded, membrane removed,
    and sliced

1 habañero chile, trimmed and sliced
    or to taste

1 jalapeño chile, trimmed and sliced
    or to taste

½ teaspoon crushed red pepper flakes
    or to taste

1 medium head green cabbage, cored
    and thinly sliced

Salt and pepper to taste

2 cups low-sodium chicken broth
    or water

2 tablespoons chopped cilantro

This is one hot mama! I've taken humdrum cabbage and added some fire. A great mix of vegetables zapped with some fresh chiles and cilantro takes this dish on a little trip south of the border.

SERVES 6

MISS PATTI'S CABBAGE SHUFFLE

1. Place a large nonstick frying pan over medium-high heat. When just hot, add the oil.

2. When the oil is hot, add the potatoes, carrots, onion, bell pepper, chiles and red pepper flakes and cook, stirring, for 2 minutes or just until very fragrant and beginning to soften. Add the cabbage, season with salt and pepper, and continue to cook, stirring, for 4 minutes.

3. Add the broth, stirring to blend. Lower the heat and cook, tossing and stirring, for about 15 minutes or until the vegetables are tender and the flavors have blended.

4. Remove from the heat, stir in the cilantro, and serve.

1 large (about 1 pound) Vidalia onion

½ cup all-purpose flour

2 teaspoons paprika

2 teaspoons cayenne pepper

1 teaspoon salt

¼ teaspoon black pepper

1 large egg

½ cup milk

Approximately 4 cups vegetable oil for frying

LaBelle Pepper Clear Mild Pepper Sauce

*T*he first time that I was served an onion blossom, I just knew that I had to figure out how to make one. They are addictive—especially when served with a hot sauce. You can now buy the little thingamajig that cuts the onion neatly, but I manage to just slice away and it seems to work. This is enough seasoning to coat 2 to 3 large onions.

SERVES 2

VIDALIA ONION BLOSSOM

1. Slice about 1-inch off the top of the onion, leaving the root end undisturbed. Carefully pull off the outer dry skin. Using a very sharp knife, cut down into the center of the onion to about half an inch from the root end and move the knife outward to make a neat cut. Repeat this process from 12 to 16 times around the onion, leaving an even space between each cut. The number of cuts will depend upon the size of the onion. Gently pull the onion to spread the cut pieces outward. Be very careful—you don't want to break off any of the pieces. The onion should now look somewhat like a big chrysanthemum.

2. Place the onion in very hot water to cover for 1 minute. Remove and place, cut side down, on a double layer of paper towel to drain.

3. Combine the flour with the paprika, cayenne, salt, and pepper in a small but deep bowl—one large enough to dip the onion into.

4. Whisk the egg and milk together in another small, deep bowl.

5. Place the oil in a small (about 8-inches in diameter), deep saucepan (or deep-fat fryer) placed over high heat. Bring to 360°F on an instant-read thermometer.

6. First carefully dip the onion into the flour, shaking off excess. Then dip it into the egg mixture, allowing excess to drip off. Again dip it into the flour to make an even coating.

7. Carefully drop the coated onion into the hot oil and fry for about 12 minutes or until golden brown and cooked through.

8. Remove from the oil and drain on a double layer of paper towel.

9. Serve with Pepper Clear sprinkled on the petals or with any hot and spicy dipping sauce.

1 tablespoon vegetable oil

1 large onion, peeled and diced

1 tablespoon minced garlic

2 pounds lean ground turkey

LaBelle Seasoned Sea Salt and Seasoned Pepper to taste

One 14½-ounce can low-sodium chicken broth

One 14½- ounce can tomato sauce

One 14½-ounce can diced tomatoes with green chiles

One 10-ounce can enchilada sauce

½ cup LaBelle Diced Fine Jalapeños

One 16-ounce can pinto beans with their juices

2½ tablespoons chili powder or to taste

Salt to taste, optional

1 cup shredded sharp Cheddar cheese

*I*t would be difficult to find a quicker and easier way than this to put a little spice in your life. The chili can be made with ground beef or pork, but I prefer the lighter turkey. No matter the meat, I always serve mine with Cornbread (see page 102) and a few bottles of hot sauce on the side.

SERVES 6 TO 8

OOH-LA-LABELLE TURKEY CHILI

44

1. Heat the oil in a large saucepan over medium-high heat. Add the onion and garlic and sauté for 2 minutes or just until softened. Add the turkey along with the seasoning salt and pepper to taste and cook, stirring frequently to break the turkey into small clumps, for about 8 minutes or until the mixture has browned nicely.

2. Add the chicken broth, tomato sauce, tomatoes and chiles, enchilada sauce, and diced jalapeños, stirring to blend. Then, stir in the beans and chili powder and bring to a simmer.

3. Taste and add salt and pepper, if necessary. Lower the heat and cook at a bare simmer for about 40 minutes or until the flavors are well blended.

4. Remove from the heat and ladle into serving bowls. Top each bowl with an equal portion of the cheese. Serve piping hot.

*2½ cups of your favorite biscuit
  mix*

1 large egg, beaten

1 cup milk

¼ cup melted butter

*¼ cup grated sharp Cheddar
  cheese*

*¼ cup grated mild Cheddar
  cheese*

¼ cup grated Parmesan cheese

*1 to 2 tablespoons LaBelle Diced
  Fine Jalapeños, or to taste*

*C*heese biscuits are good—but spicy cheese biscuits are so much better! I've gone easy on you with only a tablespoon of heat added, but don't be afraid to up the Scoville units (that's how chile pepper heat is measured) if you really want to fry your mouth!

MAKES ABOUT 1½ DOZEN

MISS PATTI'S HOT CHEESE BISCUITS

1. Preheat the oven to 425°F.

2. Place the biscuit mix in a medium mixing bowl.

3. In a separate bowl, whisk the egg into the milk. When combined, whisk in the butter and then pour it over the biscuit mix, stirring with a fork to make a soft batter.

4. Add the Cheddar and Parmesan cheeses along with the jalapeños, stirring to evenly distribute the cheeses and peppers.

5. Drop the mixture, by the tablespoonful, onto a nonstick cookie sheet, allowing about an inch between each biscuit.

6. Place in the preheated oven and bake for about 14 minutes or until golden brown and baked through.

7. Remove from the oven and serve hot.

Down-Home Stick to Your Ribs Meals

*W*hether you grew up in the South, New York City, Los Angeles, or West Philadelphia, where I grew up, you know what down-home food is. When you smell it cooking, it brings back memories and makes you feel a certain way inside.

I didn't call it down-home food when I was growing up. But I knew it was special. It was the kind of meal that made my mouth water when it hit the table. Heck, my mouth is watering right now just thinking about it! These are the meals that stick to your ribs—and, unfortunately, a lot of other places, too!

In my home, that kind of food meant love because love came from the hands that prepared it. My mother gave me her recipes, which she got from my grandmother, and which my grandmother got from my great-grandmother. Some of my recipes go back that far. And by sharing them with you, I'm making sure that they will go on forever. So sit back and bring on your appetite as I give you a taste of some down-home traditional recipes with a new Patti twist.

One of my favorites is hearty potato soup on a cold winter day. It will literally soothe your soul. I like it because it's a meal in a bowl that you can cook up in no time at all. If you're like I am and find yourself in a constant time crunch, then this is the meal for you. The best part about this soup is that you can fix it on one day and have delicious leftovers for a few days after—and it tastes even better the second day!

But it's the Bangin' Brisket that makes me hit a high note in the kitchen. I love this dish because after all the ingredients are in the pot, it cooks itself. You don't have to stand over it, watching it and stirring it. You can just leave it and let it simmer all day. (Of course, I check on it from time to time because I can't help myself.) The meat is so tender when it's done that it just melts in your mouth. I like to serve it with a side of veggies and my garlic mashed potatoes (see page 187), topped off with the beef brisket gravy. This is one of my favorite meals to cook, because it was the last thing I got to make for my dear friend, Luther Vandross. I went to visit him in the hospital before he passed and he said, "Patti, bring me some of your brisket!"

"Now Luther, are you sure you can have it?" I asked, thinking it would be too much for him. He was very weak.

"I can have it," he said. "Don't come back here without some brisket!"

He was serious, too. I asked his nurses just to be sure and they said it was fine. I came back the next day with a big ole pot. It did my heart good to see Luther have so much joy from my food. I will never forget that feeling. That's what good, down-home food can do. It didn't heal him, but it sure did make him happy.

White Bean and Collard Green Soup

Soothe Your Soul Potato Soup

Bangin' Brisket

Short Ribs in Brown Gravy

Smothered Pork Chops

Baked Blackened Catfish

Good Ole Gumbo

Spicy Southern-Fried Turkey Wings

Down-Home Fish and Chips

Salmon and Grits by Norma

Over the Top, Top, Top Macaroni and Cheese

Perfectly Seasoned Mean Greens

Fierce Fried Corn

Fried Green Tomatoes

Pickled Beets

2 tablespoons olive oil

3 cloves garlic, peeled and sliced

2 medium carrots, peeled, trimmed,
and finely diced

2 ribs celery, well-washed, peeled,
and finely diced

1 cup diced onions

Salt to taste

One 28-ounce can crushed tomatoes

1 bay leaf

2 pounds fresh collard greens, well-washed
and chopped

6 cups low-sodium chicken broth or water

Four 15.5-ounce cans cannellini beans,
well-drained

2 teaspoons freshly ground black pepper or
to taste

2 teaspoons LaBelle Pepper Clear Mild
Pepper Sauce

¼ cup grated Parmesan cheese

2 tablespoons chopped fresh flat leaf
parsley, optional

A little bit of southern soul and a little bit of Italian flair come together in this dish. Beans and greens are a favorite combo the world over, and I think that my take on it makes this soup one of the best. It really does only take a heaping pile of greens to make a meal complete.

SERVES 6

WHITE BEAN AND COLLARD GREEN SOUP

1. Place the oil in a Dutch oven over low heat. When hot, add the garlic, carrots, celery and onion. Season with salt and cook, stirring occasionally, for 5 minutes. Add the tomatoes and bay leaf, raise the heat to medium-high, and bring to a boil. Lower the heat to a bare simmer, cover, and cook for 20 minutes or until the vegetables are very tender.

2. Blanch the greens in boiling salted water for 5 minutes. Drain and cool under cold running water. Squeeze dry.

3. Add the broth and the beans, stirring to combine. Season with lots of pepper and the hot sauce. Cover and cook for about 10 minutes. Stir in the collard greens and continue cooking for another 20 minutes or until very flavorful. Taste and, if necessary, add salt and pepper.

4. Remove from the heat and pour into a soup tureen. Sprinkle with cheese and parsley, and serve piping hot.

½ cup butter

½ cup diced thick turkey bacon

1 leek, white part only, well-washed
   and chopped

1 rib celery, well-washed, dried,
   trimmed, and diced

1 teaspoon minced garlic

3 pounds Yukon gold potatoes, peeled
   and cubed

6 cups low-sodium chicken broth (or
   half broth and water)

Salt and ground white pepper to taste

2 cups heavy cream

2½ cups hot milk

1 cup sour cream

2 tablespoons finely chopped scallions
   with some green part

*T*his truly is a soothing soup. Sure, it's hearty, too—but also so smooth and mellow that it just makes you feel good on a cold, winter day.

SERVES 6

SOOTHE YOUR SOUL POTATO SOUP

54

1. Heat the butter in a large saucepan over medium heat. Add the bacon along with the leek, celery and garlic, and cook, stirring frequently, for about 5 minutes or until the bacon is crisp and the vegetables have softened and taken on some color.

2. Add the potatoes and sauté for 3 minutes or until beginning to soften. Add the broth, raise the heat, and bring to a boil. Lower the heat, season with salt and pepper, and cook at a gentle simmer for 40 minutes or until the potatoes are beginning to fall apart and the liquid has reduced to about 4 cups.

3. While the soup is cooking, place the cream in a small saucepan and bring to a simmer. Simmer, watching carefully so the cream doesn't boil over the pan, for about 20 minutes or until reduced to 1 cup.

4. Remove the soup from the heat and, in batches, carefully pour the liquid into a blender jar. Holding the lid down with a kitchen towel to keep the heat from pushing it off, process until smooth, adding hot milk as necessary to thin down.

5. Return the puréed soup to a medium saucepan. Add the reduced cream along with any remaining milk and bring to a bare simmer. Whisk in the sour cream, season with salt and pepper, and cook for a couple of minutes to heat through.

6. Remove from the heat and serve, garnished with scallions.

4 to 5 pounds beef brisket, trimmed
  of excess fat

2 tablespoons LaBelle Seasoned Pepper
  Blend or your favorite LaBelle blended
  seasoning to taste

3 tablespoons "lite" olive oil

5 cloves garlic, peeled and minced

1 large Vidalia onion, peeled and sliced

1 cup diced celery

2 cups chopped canned tomatoes, well-drained

2 cups red wine

4 cups low-sodium beef broth

2 tablespoons LaBelle Hot Flash
  Hot Sauce, or to taste

6 medium potatoes, well-washed and cut
  into quarters

3 carrots, peeled and cubed

1 cup chopped scallions with some green part

This is one of my most
favorite recipes because,
once all of the ingredients
are in the pot, it cooks
itself. I don't have to stand
over the stove, watching
and stirring, which lets
me spend more time with
friends and family. And,
once done, the meat is so
juicy and tender that it just
about melts in your mouth.

SERVES 6 TO 8

BANGIN' BRISKET

1. Preheat the oven to 350°F.

2. Season the brisket with blackening mix, rubbing it into all sides.

3. Heat the oil in a Dutch oven over medium-high heat. When very hot, add the seasoned brisket and sear one side for about 3 minutes or until brown. Turn and sear the remaining side for another 3 minutes or until brown.

4. Transfer the brisket to a platter.

5. Immediately add the garlic, onion and celery, and cook, stirring frequently, for about 4 minutes or until softened and slightly colored. Add the tomatoes, stirring to blend. Add the wine and bring to a boil. Cook, stirring, for about 4 minutes or until the wine has reduced by one quarter. Stir in the broth and, when blended, return the brisket to the pan. If the liquid does not cover the meat, add enough water to cover by 2 inches. Season with Hot Flash and again bring to a boil.

6. Cover and place in the preheated oven and bake for about 3 hours or until tender.

7. Remove from the oven and uncover. Do not turn the oven off.

8. Add the potatoes and carrots, cover, and return to the oven. Bake for another 30 minutes or until the meat is tender enough to separate with a fork.

9. Remove from the oven, uncover, and stir in the scallions.

1 cup Wondra flour

1 teaspoon garlic powder

1 teaspoon onion powder

1 teaspoon seasoned salt

5 pounds beef short ribs, trimmed of
excess fat and silverskin

1/4 cup vegetable oil

2 cloves garlic, peeled and minced

1 large onion, peeled and sliced

1 large green bell pepper, well-washed,
cored, seeded, membrane removed,
and diced

1 large carrot, peeled, trimmed, and diced

1 rib celery, peeled, trimmed, and diced

2 cups dry red wine

4 cups low-sodium beef broth

1 tablespoon tomato paste

Salt and pepper to taste

1 tablespoon cornstarch dissolved in
2 tablespoons cold water

*N*othing sticks to your ribs more than, well—ribs! I like to serve these short ribs with mashed potatoes and a mess of greens, which makes me feel like I'm home no matter where I am—even in a drafty dressing room far from Philly.

SERVES 6

SHORT RIBS IN BROWN GRAVY

1. Season the flour with the garlic and onion powders and seasoned salt. Dust the ribs with the seasoned flour, shaking off any excess.

2. Heat the oil in a Dutch oven over high heat. When almost smoking, add the ribs, a few at a time if necessary to keep from crowding the pan. Cook, turning frequently, fro about 5 minutes or until well-browned on all sides. Transfer to a platter.

3. When all of the ribs are browned, add the garlic, onion, bell pepper, carrot and celery to the pan, and cook, stirring frequently, for about 5 minutes or just until softened. Add the wine and cook, stirring, for about 5 minutes or until the brown bits are off the bottom of the pan and the alcohol has burned off.

4. Add the broth and tomato paste, stirring to blend. Return the ribs to the pan, season with salt and pepper, and bring to a boil. Lower the heat, cover, and simmer for 2 hours or until the meat is almost falling off the bones. Check the liquid level from time to time to make certain that the ribs remain submerged. If not, add a bit more broth or water.

5. Uncover the ribs and stir in the cornstarch mixture. Cook, stirring constantly, for about 3 minutes or until the gravy has thickened.

6. Remove from the heat and serve.

½ cup all-purpose flour

1 tablespoon garlic powder

1 tablespoon onion powder

1 teaspoon paprika

1 teaspoon cayenne pepper

Salt to taste

Six 6-ounce boneless pork chops, trimmed of all fat

2 tablespoons butter

1 medium onion, peeled and cut into slivers

½ cup diced turkey bacon

One 8-ounce package button mushrooms, cleaned and thinly sliced

2 tablespoons vegetable oil

1 cup buttermilk

1 cup heavy cream

1 tablespoon parsley, optional

The Southwest has chicken-fried steak—well, down-home we have the next best thing: smothered pork chops. Here I use boneless chops (you can use bone-in, if you prefer) nestled in creamy gravy—it's perfect for soppin' up with some buttermilk biscuits. The addition of fresh mushrooms takes this from the kitchen table to the dining room.

SERVES 6

SMOTHERED PORK CHOPS

1. Combine the flour with the garlic and onion powders, paprika and cayenne pepper, and salt to taste in a large shallow bowl. Working with one at a time, press the chops into the seasoned flour, making sure that they are well-coated. Shake off excess flour and set the chops aside.

2. Heat the butter in a frying pan large enough to snugly fit the pork chops. When the butter starts to foam, add the onion and bacon and fry, stirring frequently, for about 2 minutes or just until the onion has wilted. Stir in the mushrooms and fry, stirring occasionally, for another 4 minutes or until the mushrooms have begun to exude their liquid and the onions have colored. Scrape the mixture from the pan into a bowl and set aside.

3. Wipe the pan clean with a paper towel and return it to medium heat. Add the oil and when very hot, add the chops. Sear for about 2 minutes or until nicely colored and then turn and sear the remaining side for 2 minutes or until nicely colored.

4. Add the reserved mushroom mixture to the pan. Pour in the buttermilk and cream and bring to a simmer. Lower the heat, cover with the lid slightly ajar, and cook at a bare simmer for about 15 minutes or until the gravy has thickened and the chops are cooked through. Taste and, if necessary, add salt and pepper.

5. Remove from the heat and serve, sprinkled with parsley, if desired.

3 tablespoons olive oil

3 cloves garlic, peeled and thinly
     sliced

2 small shallots, peeled and
     thinly sliced

2 tablespoons chopped cilantro

2 teaspoons lime juice

Six 6-ounce skinless catfish fillets

3 tablespoons LaBelle Seasoned
     Pepper Blend or your favorite
     LaBelle blended seasoning to
     taste

1 cup fine yellow cornmeal

1 teaspoon salt

¼ cup "lite" olive oil

2 tablespoons melted butter

Lime wedges for serving, optional

*C*atfish is a down-home favorite. I love to bake it with a crunchy cornmeal crust and then serve it up with some greens (see page 74) and Spicy Dirty Rice (see page 38). And, of course, there's nothing wrong with having hot sauce on the table to add some heat to the mix.

SERVES 6

BAKED BLACKENED CATFISH

1. Combine the olive oil with the garlic, shallots, cilantro and lime juice in a small mixing bowl, stirring to blend.

2. Place the catfish in a single layer in a shallow dish large enough to hold them. Pour the olive oil mix over the top and set aside for 15 minutes.

3. Preheat the oven to 350°F.

4. Lightly coat the interior of a baking dish large enough to hold the six fillets in a single layer with nonstick vegetable spray. Set aside.

5. Combine the cornmeal with the spice mix and salt in a shallow bowl, stirring to blend.

6. Remove the fish from the marinade and allow excess to drip off. Strain the marinade, reserving the liquid.

7. Carefully dredge both sides of each fillet in the cornmeal mix.

8. Place a large cast-iron skillet over high heat. When almost smoking, add the "lite" oil and butter. Carefully place 3 of the fillets into the pan. Sear for 2 minutes and then turn and sear the remaining side for 2 minutes.

9. Carefully transfer the seared fish to the prepared baking dish. Then, sear the remaining 3 fillets and, when seared, place them in the prepared dish.

10. Place in the preheated oven and bake for 7 minutes or until the fish flakes easily when pierced with a fork.

11. Remove from the oven and serve with lime wedges, if desired.

¼ cup "lite" olive oil

3 cloves garlic, peeled and minced

2 ribs celery, well-washed, peeled, and diced

1 medium onion, peeled and chopped

¼ cup all-purpose flour

1 pound andouille or other smoked sausage, cut into bite-sized pieces

½ pound okra, washed, trimmed, and cut, crosswise, into bite-sized pieces

2 cups chicken broth

1 cup bottled clam juice

One 28-ounce can chopped tomatoes with their juice

1¼ cups thawed frozen corn kernels

2 tablespoons LaBelle Seasoned Pepper Blend or your favorite LaBelle blended seasoning to taste

1 tablespoon LaBelle Rich Red Hot Sauce

1 pound catfish or tilapia fillets, cut into 1-inch pieces

1 pound cooked medium shrimp, peeled and deveined

1 pound cooked crawdads, cleaned

½ tablespoon file powder or to taste

¼ cup chopped parsley

6 to 8 cups hot cooked rice, optional

I've gone easy on the heat, but for a real Big Easy hit, just keep adding that cayenne or some hot sauce. And, while you're at it, you might as well triple the recipe 'cause everybody will ask for seconds and thirds! Fresh okra makes all the difference in this recipe, but if you can't find it, just substitute frozen okra.

SERVES 6 TO 8

GOOD OLE GUMBO

1. Heat the oil in a large heavy bottomed saucepan over medium-high heat. When very hot, stir in the garlic, celery and onion. Cook, stirring frequently, for about 4 minutes or until softened and lightly colored. Stir in the flour and cook, stirring constantly, for about 4 minutes or until the flour has begun to color.

2. Add the sausage and okra and cook, stirring frequently, for about 3 minutes or until the sausage releases some of its fat.

3. Add the broth and clam juice and bring to a boil. Lower the heat and simmer for about 15 minutes or until the liquid has reduced by half. Stir in the tomatoes along with their juices and again bring to a boil. Lower the heat and simmer for 15 minutes. Then, stir in the corn, blackened spice and hot sauce. Taste and, if necessary, adjust the seasoning with salt and cayenne. Bring to a simmer, then simmer for 20 minutes or until thickened.

4. Add the diced fish and cook for 5 minutes. Stir in the shrimp and crawdads and again bring to a simmer. Simmer for 3 more minutes or until very hot.

5. Stir in the file powder and chopped parsley and, if desired, serve with rice.

8 turkey wings, tips removed

¾ cup Miss Patti's Spice Blend (recipe follows)

½ cup LaBelle Hot Flash Hot Sauce

2 cups all-purpose flour

Paprika to taste

Cayenne pepper to taste

Seasoned salt and ground black pepper to taste

Approximately 2 quarts peanut oil for frying

*I*f you have an outdoor fryer, this recipe will give it a good workout. Once you've made these hot, hot, hot turkey wings, little ole puny chicken wings won't quite cut it. But, the smaller wings do make better snack food, while the meaty turkey wings make a whole meal.

I'm also sharing my secret spice blend— I've given you the recipe to make 4 cups so you have some extra on hand to add zest to everyday meals. Just a sprinkle will add sparkle!

SERVES 6 TO 8

SPICY SOUTHERN-FRIED TURKEY WINGS

1. Using a sharp knife, cut each wing into 2 pieces, the drumette and the second joint. Rinse under cold, running water and pat dry.

2. Place the wings in a large bowl. Add ½ cup of the spice blend and toss to coat. Transfer the seasoned wings to extra-large, resealable plastic bags (you might need 3 or 4). Add the Hot Flash, seal the bag, forcing out as much of the air as possible, and push the wings around to evenly coat. (Alternately, you can do the marinating in a large bowl or baking dish, covered with plastic film.)

3. Place the wings in the refrigerator to marinate for at least 2 hours or overnight.

4. When ready to cook, place the flour along with the remaining 2 tablespoons of spice blend, paprika, cayenne, and salt and pepper in an extra-large, resealable plastic bag. Add the seasoned salt and pepper, seal, and shake to combine.

5. Remove the wings from the refrigerator and transfer them to the flour mixture. Seal the bag and toss to evenly coat the wings with the seasoned flour.

6. Place the oil in a deep fat fryer fitted with the basket insert over high heat, heating to 360°F on an instant-read thermometer.

7. Remove the wings from the flour, shaking off any excess. Place the wings, a couple at a time, into the hot oil and fry for about 16 minutes or until golden brown and cooked through (the juices will run clear when the wings are poked with the tip of a small, sharp knife). Extra large wings will take a few minutes longer. (You can, if you prefer, brown and crisp the wings in deep fat and then drain well and transfer to baking pans, in a single layer, and finish the cooking in a preheated 350°F oven.)

8. Lift the wings from the hot oil and place on a double layer of paper towel to drain.

9. Serve hot with Hot Flash on the side for adding fuel to the fire.

Miss Patti's Spice Blend

Combine the seasoned salt, garlic and onion powders, and seasoned pepper in a small mixing bowl. When well-combined, transfer to a quart jar with a tight lid. Cover and store in a cool, dry spot.

1 cup LaBelle Seasoned Sea Salt

1 cup garlic powder

1 cup onion powder

1 cup LaBelle Seasoned Pepper

½ cup "lite" olive oil

4 medium potatoes, peeled and cut
    into ¼-inch thick sticks

1 teaspoon salt

1 teaspoon freshly ground black pepper

2 teaspoons paprika

¼ teaspoon onion powder

¼ teaspoon dried parsley flakes

Six 6-ounce flounder or other white
    fish fillets

1 teaspoon garlic powder

¼ teaspoon dried rosemary

1 cup fine breadcrumbs

1 teaspoon lemon juice

Lemon wedges, optional

Who would have guessed that down-home could be so good for you. No fish fry here—just some olive oil, great seasoning, and a hot oven to make a crisp mix of potatoes and fish. No greasy papers and no ketchup, but this is a case where "less is more."

SERVES 6

DOWN-HOME FISH AND CHIPS

1. Preheat the oven to 350°F.

2. Using ¼ cup of the olive oil, lightly coat 2 rimmed baking sheets. Set aside.

3. Place the potatoes in a resealable plastic bag. Add ¼ cup of the oil along with half of the salt and pepper and the paprika, onion powder, and parsley. Seal the bag and toss the bag around to coat the potatoes with the oil and seasonings.

4. Transfer the potatoes to one of the prepared baking sheets. Place in the preheated oven and bake for 1 hour or until crisp, golden brown, and tender.

5. Thirty minutes into the baking of the potatoes, season the fish with the remaining salt and pepper along with the garlic powder and rosemary.

6. Place the breadcrumbs on a plate and, working with one piece at a time, lightly dredge each fish fillet in the breadcrumbs.

7. Place the coated fish on the remaining rimmed baking sheet and drizzle lemon juice over the top.

8. Place in the preheated oven along with the potatoes and bake for about 10 minutes or until the fish flakes easily when pierced with a fork.

9. Remove the potatoes and fish from the oven and serve with lemon wedges on the side.

6 cups salted water

1 cup yellow cornmeal

½ tablespoon paprika

Pinch cayenne pepper

Six 6-ounce skinless salmon fillets, cut in half, crosswise

2 teaspoons LaBelle Seasoned Sea Salt, or to taste

½ teaspoon LaBelle Seasoned Pepper, or to taste

¼ cup butter, cut into pieces

1 cup plus 2 tablespoons quick-cooking grits

¼ cup half-and-half

3 tablespoons "lite" olive oil

1 tablespoon chopped cilantro or parsley

Fish and grits—another down-home staple. But this is a healthy spin on a favorite. I love to throw this meal together after a long day of work. This dish is normally prepared with fried whiting, but by substituting "good for you salmon" and pan-frying it instead of deep-frying, you have a healthier alternative and won't sacrifice a bit of taste!

SERVES 6

SALMON AND GRITS BY NORMA

1. Place the cornmeal, paprika, and cayenne on a large plate. Set aside.

2. Season the salmon with seasoning salt and seasoning pepper to taste. Then, dredge both sides in the cornmeal mixture.

3. Place 6 cups of salted water in a medium saucepan over high heat. Add the butter and bring to a boil. Immediately stir in the grits and return to a boil. Lower the heat and cook, stirring frequently, for about 8 minutes or until just about cooked and quite thick. If the grits get too thick before they are cooked, add a bit of water.

4. Add the half-and-half, beating to blend. Return the grits to a simmer and then turn off the heat. Cover and let stand while you prepare the salmon.

5. About 10 minutes before the grits are ready, prepare the salmon.

6. Heat the oil in a large nonstick frying pan over medium-high heat.

7. When very hot, but not smoking, add the salmon and cook, turning once, for about 4 minutes or until just barely cooked in the center.

8. Remove from the heat and place on a double layer of paper towel to drain.

9. Spoon an equal portion of the grits into the center of each of six dinner plates. Place 2 pieces of salmon on the top of each portion. Sprinkle with cilantro and serve.

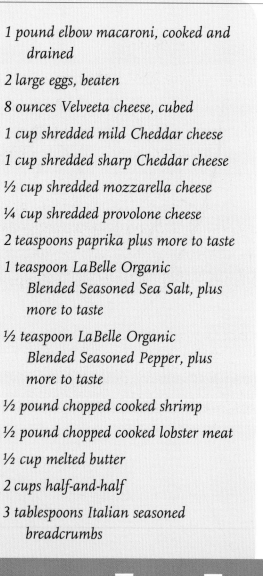

1 pound elbow macaroni, cooked and
   drained

2 large eggs, beaten

8 ounces Velveeta cheese, cubed

1 cup shredded mild Cheddar cheese

1 cup shredded sharp Cheddar cheese

½ cup shredded mozzarella cheese

¼ cup shredded provolone cheese

2 teaspoons paprika plus more to taste

1 teaspoon LaBelle Organic
   Blended Seasoned Sea Salt, plus
   more to taste

½ teaspoon LaBelle Organic
   Blended Seasoned Pepper, plus
   more to taste

½ pound chopped cooked shrimp

½ pound chopped cooked lobster meat

½ cup melted butter

2 cups half-and-half

3 tablespoons Italian seasoned
   breadcrumbs

I don't know if you folks
have ever had a macaroni and
cheese quite like this one. It's
truly over the top and back
around again. I know it sounds
like a lot of flavors clashing, but
once you've tried it, you'll never
go back to that old, tired box
mix. Trust Miss Patti, I know
my mac 'n' cheese!

SERVES 6 TO 8

OVER THE TOP, TOP, TOP
MACARONI AND CHEESE

1. Preheat the oven to 350°F.

2. Lightly butter the interior of a 2½ quart casserole dish.

3. Place the cooked macaroni and eggs in a mixing bowl, stirring to coat well.

4. Add the Velveeta, Cheddar cheeses, mozzarella, and provolone cheeses to the macaroni, stirring to blend well. Season with 2 teaspoons paprika, 1 teaspoon seasoning salt, and ½ teaspoon seasoning pepper, stirring to blend. Pour the mixture into the prepared casserole dish.

5. Make a layer of shrimp followed by a layer of lobster. Pour the melted butter over all and season the top with paprika, salt and pepper. Pour the half-and-half over the top and sprinkle with breadcrumbs.

6. Using a paper towel, clean off the interior of the casserole dish so it doesn't burn.

7. Place in the preheated oven and bake for about 25 minutes or until golden brown and bubbling.

8. Remove from the heat and serve.

2 pounds smoked turkey necks

2 tablespoons minced garlic

2 tablespoons minced shallots

1 teaspoon freshly ground black pepper

8 bunches collard greens, well-washed and cut into 1-inch pieces

Nothing says "home" like a mess of greens cooking on the back burner. Oh, that smell just pulls you to the table. I know because I've eaten more than my share.

My one bit of advice—wash the greens, then wash them again, and wash them once more for good measure, until the water is sparkling clean. You don't want any grit in your greens!

SERVES 6

PERFECTLY SEASONED MEAN GREENS

1. Place the turkey necks in a large pot with cold water to cover by 2-inches. Place over high heat and bring to a boil. Lower the heat and simmer for about 1½ hours or until the meat is falling off of the bone. If necessary, add more water to keep the hocks well covered with liquid.

2. Add the garlic, shallots and pepper, stirring to blend. Begin adding the greens in batches. As they wilt, add more until all of the greens are in the pot. Raise the heat and bring to a boil. Lower the heat and cook at a gentle simmer, stirring occasionally, for 30 to 45 minutes or until the greens are very tender. About halfway through the cooking, taste and, if necessary, add salt and pepper to taste. Remove from the heat and serve—with cornbread for the real deal.

*I*f you don't have a fresh chile on hand, just substitute LaBelle Diced Fine Jalapeños in whatever amount pleases your palate. As you know, hot is never really hot enough for me, so I might just add some more once the corn is on my plate.

SERVES 6

¼ cup butter

½ cup finely diced onions

½ cup finely diced red bell pepper

Kernels from 8 ears fresh corn, about 4 cups

2 tablespoons LaBelle Diced Fine Jalapeños, or to taste

Salt and ground black pepper to taste

2 tablespoons chopped scallions with some green part

FIERCE FRIED CORN

1. Heat the butter in a large nonstick frying pan over low heat. Add the onions and bell pepper and cook, stirring, for 3 minutes or just until softened. Add the corn and jalapeños, season with salt and pepper to taste, and cook, stirring constantly, for about 7 minutes or until the corn is tender.

2. Remove from the heat, stir in the scallions, and serve.

2 large eggs or the equivalent egg
replacement

½ cup 2% milk

1 tablespoon LaBelle Rich Red Hot
Sauce, or to taste

1 cup all-purpose flour

¼ cup cornmeal

Salt and pepper to taste

¼ cup vegetable oil

5 large green tomatoes, well-washed,
cored, and cut crosswise into
½-inch thick slices

*I*t used to be that you could only make these in the summer when the vines were overloaded with tomatoes—but nowadays, winter tomatoes are so firm and almost tasteless that I find they are great for frying. Fried tomatoes can be served anytime—they are a terrific side dish for breakfast or brunch, and they also make a great sandwich with crisp turkey bacon.

SERVES 6

FRIED GREEN TOMATOES

1. Combine the eggs, milk and hot sauce in a shallow bowl.

2. Combine the flour, cornmeal and salt and pepper to taste in another shallow bowl.

3. Heat the oil in a large, nonstick frying pan over medium heat. When hot, begin dipping the tomato slices in the egg mixture and then the flour. Shake off excess and place the coated tomatoes into the hot oil. This may have to be done in batches with fresh oil each time.

4. Fry for about 1 minute and turn. Fry for another minute or so or until the tomatoes are golden brown and the coating is crisp.

5. Remove from the pan and serve with more Rich Red on the side.

These are great to cook up and keep on hand for a last-minute veggie. You can toss some in a green salad or pasta salad, put a few on a sandwich, or just eat them out of the bowl. Don't you just love sweet, spicy, sour dishes that can jazz up almost anything?

SERVES 6

2 pounds cooked beets, peeled and sliced

1 large red onion

¼ cup LaBelle Sweet Hot Jalapeño Relish, or to taste

1 cup cider vinegar

2 tablespoons sugar

¼ teaspoons celery seeds, optional

Salt and pepper to taste

PICKLED BEETS

Combine the beets with the onion and relish in a mixing bowl, stirring to combine. Add the vinegar, sugar, celery seeds and salt and pepper to taste, and stir to combine. Cover and refrigerate for at least 2 hours or up to one week before serving, chilled.

Light & Healthy
(But It Still Tastes Great!)

I love life! And what I've discovered is that life is a whole lot better when I feel good. As you know, after a few health scares, I had to change how I eat. I had to find ways to make my meals so that I could enjoy my food and not pay for it later. If you grew up the way I did, good food was all about those meals that "stick to your ribs" and that make you sleepy when you eat them—meat and potatoes, rich gravies and loads of fats. But when you know better, you do better.

So, I had to switch it up. The multiple pats of butter were replaced with olive oil, the deep-frying was replaced with pan searing, and the heaps of sugar were replaced with sugar substitutes. Fortunately, I didn't lose the flavor in the process of making these changes. I did a whole cookbook dedicated to this kind of eating in *Patti Labelle's Lite Cuisine: 100 Dishes with To-Die-For Taste Made With To-Live-For Recipes.* Here are a few more special recipes to add to the mix, like my Hot and Sassy Gazpacho and my Jerk Seasoned Chicken and Pepper Sauté. And if you want a burger, well I've got you covered on that too. "Where's the beef?"—you don't need it. My turkey burger will satisfy you and you won't miss the meat one bit.

LIGHT VEGETABLE SOUP WITH CHICKEN

HOT AND SASSY GAZPACHO

GENTLE LENTIL, CHICKEN & BARLEY SOUP

QUICK AND EASY PORK TENDERLOIN

TURKEY BURGERS

GRILLED CHICKEN BREASTS WITH
PICO DE GALLO

JERK SEASONED CHICKEN
AND PEPPER SAUTÉ

BROILED SNAPPER WITH HERBS

GRILLED MIXED VEGETABLES

SAUTÉED OKRA, CORN & TOMATOES

OVEN-BAKED FRIES

SHRIMP & CELERY SALAD

THREE BEAN SALAD

AS GOOD AS IT GETS CORNBREAD

WATERMELON COOLER

2 tablespoons vegetable oil

3 ribs celery, well-washed, peeled, and cut, crosswise, into thin slices

2 medium potatoes, peeled and diced

2 medium carrots, peeled, trimmed and diced

2 medium zucchini, well-washed, trimmed, and diced

2 cloves garlic, peeled and minced

1 onion, peeled and diced

1 green bell pepper, well-washed, cored, seeded, membrane removed, and diced

1 cup sliced button mushrooms

Two 46-ounce cans low-sodium vegetable broth

1½ cups carrot juice, fresh or canned

Salt and pepper to taste

4 cups torn spinach leaves or baby spinach

3 cups diced cooked chicken breast

1 cup tiny broccoli florets

*S*tarting with a base of vegetable broth and carrot juice ensures deep vegetable flavor. The chicken should just be an accent—the veggies are the real stars of this show. If you take time to cut all of the vegetables into the same size, the soup will be as pretty as a picture.

This is a great main course lunch dish served with a beautiful salad and toasted garlic bread.

SERVES 6

LIGHT VEGETABLE SOUP WITH CHICKEN

1. Heat the oil in a large soup pot over medium-high heat. Add the celery, potatoes, carrots, zucchini, garlic, onion, bell pepper and mushrooms. Cook, stirring, for about 5 minutes or until the vegetables have softened.

2. Add the vegetable broth and carrot juice and bring to a boil. Lower the heat, season with salt and pepper, and cook at a gentle simmer for about 30 minutes or until all of the vegetables are just tender.

3. Stir in the spinach, chicken and broccoli. Raise the heat and bring to a simmer. Lower the heat and continue to simmer, stirring occasionally, for 5 minutes. Taste and, if necessary, season with more salt and pepper.

4. Remove from the heat and serve.

2 pounds ripe tomatoes, peeled, cored, seeded, and coarsely chopped

1 seedless cucumber, peeled and coarsely chopped

1 red onion, peeled and coarsely chopped

1 medium green bell pepper, well-washed, cored, seeded, membrane removed, and coarsely chopped

1 tablespoon LaBelle Diced Fine Jalapeños

1 tablespoon chopped cilantro

2 teaspoons chopped parsley

1 teaspoon minced garlic

1½ cups low-sodium tomato juice

⅛ cup red wine vinegar

¼ cup extra-virgin olive oil

2 teaspoons LaBelle Seasoned Sea Salt

*G*azpacho is one of my favorite soups. Not only is it refreshing and delicious, but it can be made in just a few minutes if you use the food processor to chop the veggies. If you do, take care not to purée them, or they'll lose their crunch. I find that the crisp, fresh taste is heightened by the heat of the jalapeños. I usually add a couple of hits of my Hot Flash just before serving, but I'll leave the hot flashing up to you!

SERVES 6

HOT AND SASSY GAZPACHO

Combine the tomatoes, cucumber, onion, bell pepper and garlic in a mixing bowl. Stir in the jalapeños, cilantro, parsley and garlic. When blended, add the juice, vinegar and olive oil. Season with salt, cover, and refrigerate for at least 2 hours before serving.

*I*f you really, really clean the chicken, you'll find hardly a trace of fat in this soup. It's filled with nutrition, fiber, great flavor, and can feed a crowd to boot! When I feel extravagant, I use chicken broth as the liquid, but water or half broth with water will work just fine. You can leave the chicken on the bone or pick the meat off and return it to the pot—the first method is very simple and the latter is a bit fancier. Either way, add a big tossed salad and some chilled wine or iced tea, and you have a perfect meal.

SERVES 8 TO 10

10 chicken pieces, such as a mix of breast, legs, and thighs, all skin and fat removed, well-rinsed and patted dry

2 teaspoons LaBelle Seasoned Pepper Blend or your favorite LaBelle blended seasoning to taste

Cayenne pepper to taste

Sea salt and ground black pepper to taste

3 tablespoons "lite" olive oil

4 ribs celery, well-washed, trimmed, and diced

3 cloves garlic, peeled and minced

2 medium carrots, peeled, trimmed and diced

2 Vidalia or other sweet onions, peeled and diced

One 28-ounce can crushed tomatoes

4 quarts chicken broth or water

1 cup lentils

1 cup barley

1 teaspoon celery seed

1 cup diced yellow onion

¼ cup chopped fresh parsley

GENTLE LENTIL, CHICKEN & BARLEY SOUP

(continued)

1. Generously season the chicken with the seasoning, cayenne, sea salt and pepper. Heat the oil in a large (10 quart) soup pot over high heat. Add the seasoned chicken and sear, turning frequently, for about 5 minutes or until nicely colored on all sides.

2. Add the celery, garlic, carrots and Vidalia onions, stirring to evenly distribute. Lower the heat and cook, stirring occasionally, for another 3 minutes or just until the vegetables have begun to soften. Stir in the tomatoes, broth (or water), lentils, barley and celery seed, stirring to blend. Bring to a boil, then lower the heat and cook at a bare simmer, stirring occasionally, for about 1 hour or until the chicken is almost falling off the bone and the soup is very thick. If necessary, add a bit of water if the soup gets too thick and begins to stick to the bottom of the pot before the soup is ready.

3. About 10 minutes before the soup has finished cooking, heat some oil in a medium sauté pan over medium-high heat. Add the yellow onion and parsley and cook, stirring frequently, for about 10 minutes or until the onion is golden and beginning to crisp. Remove from the heat and drain on a double layer of paper towel.

4. Remove the soup from the heat and stir in the sautéed onion and parsley. Serve hot.

5. Store any leftovers in a covered container, refrigerated, for up to 3 days or frozen for up to 3 months.

¼ cup "lite" teriyaki sauce

¼ cup peach apricot glaze

2 tablespoons sesame oil

2 tablespoons rice wine vinegar

1 tablespoon light brown sugar

1 teaspoon crushed red pepper flakes

Two 1½-pound pork tenderloins, all silverskin and excess fat removed

2 teaspoons Kosher salt

2 teaspoons garlic powder

1 teaspoon onion powder

½ teaspoon ground black pepper

2 tablespoons canola oil

*P*ork tenderloins are so quick and easy to cook—plus, they are incredibly tender and almost fat-free. The Asian basting sauce adds interesting flavors to this mild tasting meat, which makes this a perfect celebratory dish.

SERVES 6

QUICK AND EASY PORK TENDERLOIN

1. Preheat the oven to 375°F.

2. Combine the teriyaki sauce, glaze, sesame oil, vinegar, sugar and red pepper flakes in a small mixing bowl, whisking to blend completely. Set aside.

3. Season the tenderloins with salt, garlic powder, onion powder and pepper.

(continued)

4. Heat the oil in a large ovenproof skillet over high heat. Add the seasoned tenderloins and cook, turning occasionally, for about 3 minutes or until nicely colored on all sides.

5. Remove the pan from the heat and generously coat the tenderloins with the teriyaki mixture.

6. Transfer to the preheated oven and roast, basting with the marinade at least twice, for about 30 minutes or until an instant-read thermometer inserted into the thickest part reads 160°F.

7. Remove from the oven and let rest for 5 minutes before cutting crosswise into ¼-inch thick slices.

This is a great way to enjoy a taste of Thanksgiving throughout the year. I love the sweet-tart flavor that the dried cranberries add to the meat. Lean ground turkey can be pretty dry, but I think that my additions make these burgers as tasty as a juicy, beef burger. If you want a special spread to complete the burgers, just mix a couple of tablespoons of cranberry jelly and my LaBelle Sweet Hot Jalapeño Relish with some mayo, and you're good to go.

SERVES 6

2 teaspoons canola oil

⅛ cup minced onions

1 tablespoon minced parsley

2 teaspoons poultry seasoning

2 pounds lean ground turkey

1 large egg white

½ cup dried cranberries

½ cup crushed stuffing mix

Coarse salt and freshly ground pepper to taste

LaBelle Pepper Clear Mild Pepper Sauce to taste

6 toasted hamburger buns

TURKEY BURGERS

1. Preheat and oil the grill.

2. Heat the oil in a small sauté pan over medium heat. Add the onions, parsley, and poultry seasoning and sauté for about 3 minutes or until the onions are soft. Remove from the heat.

3. Place the turkey in a mixing bowl. Add the egg white and, using your hands, squeeze to blend. Add the cranberries and stuffing mix along with the onion mix and, again using your hands, mix well to blend. Season with salt, pepper, and hot sauce to taste. Form the mix into 6 patties of equal size.

4. Place the burgers on the grill and grill for 6 minutes. Turn and grill for another 5 minutes for well done. You want the meat to be cooked through, but take care not to overcook, as the lean turkey will very quickly dry out.

3 large ripe tomatoes, peeled,
   cored, and seeded

1 medium red onion, peeled
   and cut into chunks

2 cloves garlic, peeled

1 cup cilantro leaves

Juice of 2 limes

1½ tablespoons LaBelle Diced
   Fine Jalapeños

1 teaspoon salt plus more to taste

6 boneless, skinless chicken breast
   halves

2 tablespoons canola oil

1 teaspoon chili powder

Cracked black pepper to taste

*T*his is my version of the classic salsa served with chips. You can add and subtract ingredients to make it your own—scallions instead of red onion, a few corn kernels, tomatillos in place of, or in addition to, the tomatoes—you name it, it can be yours alone.

SERVES 6

GRILLED CHICKEN BREASTS WITH PICO DE GALLO

1. Place the tomatoes, onion, garlic and cilantro in the bowl of a food processor fitted with the metal blade. Process, using quick on and off turns, for a minute or so or just until coarsely chopped.

2. Scrape the mixture from the processor bowl into a clean container. Stir in the juice of 1 lime along with the jalapeños and 1 teaspoon of salt. Cover and refrigerate until ready to serve.

3. Oil and preheat the grill.

4. Rub the chicken with the oil and the juice of the remaining lime. Season with chili powder and salt and cracked pepper to taste. Place on the preheated grill, and grill, turning occasionally, for about 10 minutes or until nicely charred and cooked through.

5. Remove from the grill and place on a serving platter. Spoon the salsa over the top and serve the remaining salsa on the side.

½ cup orange juice

2 teaspoons LaBelle Pepper Clear Mild Pepper Sauce

2 teaspoons cornstarch

2½ pounds boneless, skinless chicken breasts cut into 3-inch by ½-inch thick strips

2 tablespoons Caribbean jerk seasoning

1 teaspoon black pepper

½ teaspoon cayenne pepper or to taste

3 cloves garlic, peeled and chopped

2 large green bell peppers, well-washed, cored, seeded, membrane removed,and cut, lengthwise, into thin strips

1 large yellow bell pepper, well-washed, cored, seeded, membrane removed,and cut, lengthwise, into thin strips

1 large onion, peeled and cut, lengthwise, into thin strips

You can make this dish as hot as you like—my Pepper Clear pepper sauce is mild, so if you really want to start a fire, move up to the LaBelle Hot Flash Hot Sauce. Some sweet jasmine or basmati rice would be the perfect way to soften the intense flavors of this low-cal dish.

SERVES 6

JERK SEASONED CHICKEN AND PEPPER SAUTÉ

1. Combine the orange juice, Pepper Clear and cornstarch in a small bowl, stirring with a fork to dissolve the cornstarch. Set aside.

2. Season the chicken with jerk seasoning, black pepper and cayenne.

3. Spray a large nonstick frying pan with nonstick vegetable spray and place over medium-high heat. As soon as the pan is hot, add the seasoned chicken.

4. Cook, stirring frequently, for about 4 minutes or just until the chicken is no longer pink. Add the garlic, green and yellow peppers, and onion, stirring and tossing to blend. Cook, stirring frequently, for about 10 minutes or until the chicken is cooked through and the vegetables are crisp-tender.

5. Give the reserved orange juice mixture a quick stir and pour it into the pan, stirring to blend. Cook, stirring constantly, for about 2 minutes or until the sauce has thickened and the starchy taste has cooked out.

6. Remove from the heat and serve.

3 cloves garlic, peeled and slivered

1 small onion, peeled and thinly
sliced

2 tablespoons chopped fresh
rosemary

2 tablespoons chopped fresh
thyme

1 teaspoon cracked black pepper

¼ cup olive oil

Six 6-ounce skin-on red snapper
fillets

1 teaspoon paprika

1 tablespoon chopped flat leaf
parsley

Lemon wedges for serving,
optional

*T*here is nothing like a heap of fresh herbs to add zest without calories. Red snapper can really hold its own against the aromatic herbs, but you can prepare almost any fish using this same method. Thick fish steaks will just take a bit longer to bake.

This is a great meal to serve when the girls are getting together for lunch—you know someone is always on a diet, and this dish will satisfy everyone without putting on an extra pound.

SERVES 6

BROILED SNAPPER WITH HERBS

1. Combine the garlic, onion, rosemary, thyme and pepper with the olive oil in a small bowl.

2. Place the fish in a baking dish large enough to hold the fillets in a single layer. Pour the herb marinade over the top, spreading it out to evenly coat. Cover with plastic film and refrigerate for 2 hours.

3. Preheat the broiler to high.

4. Remove the fish from the refrigerator. Uncover, turn the fish skin-side-up, and pick off any of the garlic or onion pieces on top and push them underneath (because if you leave them on, they'll burn!). Sprinkle the top of the each fillet with paprika and season with salt to taste.

5. Place under the preheated broiler and broil, watching carefully, for about 7 minutes or until the skin has crisped and the fish is cooked through. There is no need to turn the fish because it will cook through from the top. The fish will just barely be cooked at this point; if you want a well-done fish, cook for about 3 to 5 minutes more, but do not overcook or the fish will be dry.

6. Remove from the broiler, sprinkle with parsley, and serve with lemon wedges, if desired.

3 portobello mushrooms, cleaned with stems
  removed

2 red bell peppers, well-washed, cored,
  seeded, membrane removed, and cut,
  lengthwise, into sixths

2 green bell peppers, well-washed, cored,
  seeded, membrane removed, and cut,
  lengthwise, into sixths

1 pound asparagus, well-washed and
  trimmed

1 cup balsamic vinegar

1 cup olive oil, extra-virgin if you have it

1 tablespoon chopped fresh herbs or
  1 teaspoon dried—any you like—
  I use basil or thyme

1 teaspoon minced garlic

Coarse salt and coarse ground black pepper
  to taste

This is a basic dish that allows you to mix vegetables in whatever combination you like—eggplant, tomatoes, zucchini, yellow squash, red onion, and even okra are great on the grill. Once summer passes and the backyard is a bit on the chilly side, I use a stovetop grill pan to grill my veggies, chicken breast and fish—try to pick one up, because it's an invaluable tool for cooking "lite" throughout the year.

SERVES 6

GRILLED MIXED VEGETABLES

1. Place all of the vegetables on a large platter. Add the vinegar, oil, herbs and garlic. Season with salt and pepper to taste. Using your hands, gently toss the vegetables to coat them evenly. Set aside to marinate for at least an hour or up to 8 hours.

2. Oil and preheat the grill.

3. In batches, place the vegetables on the hot grill and grill, turning frequently, long enough to tenderize the vegetable and give it some nice grill flavor and markings. Each vegetable will require a different time, depending upon its thickness and the heat of the grill. The whole process shouldn't take more than 10 or 15 minutes.

4. Remove from the grill and serve warm or at room temperature.

2 teaspoons corn oil

1 cup diced onion

2 cups diced tomatoes
(canned are fine, just
drain them well)

2 cups fresh corn kernels
(thawed, frozen are fine)

1 pound okra, well-washed,
trimmed, and cut,
crosswise, into thick slices

Seasoned salt and black
pepper to taste

This is a simple sauté that my mom used to make with bacon and bacon fat. As if that weren't enough, she even added a little heavy cream when she had it in the house. I've made it my own by lightening it up and shortening the cooking time a bit. If you like, you can add about ½ cup of chopped crisp turkey bacon just before serving.

SERVES 6

SAUTÉED OKRA, CORN & TOMATOES

Heat the oil in a large nonstick frying pan over medium heat. Add the onion and cook, stirring frequently, for about 2 minutes or just until the onions have softened. Add the tomatoes and corn and continue to cook, stirring occasionally, for about 4 minutes or just until the corn is beginning to get tender. Stir in the okra and the salt and pepper and cook for another 4 minutes. Do not overcook, or the okra will begin to ooze the gluey juices. Remove from the heat and serve with LaBelle Pepper Clear Mild Pepper Sauce.

*S*ince I, like almost everyone I know, try to watch my weight, I discovered that this method of *baking* "fries" really satisfies my longing for the standard without the addition of all the calories from the frying.

SERVES 6

6 Idaho potatoes

3 tablespoons canola or olive oil

1 teaspoon chili powder

Kosher salt and black pepper to taste

OVEN-BAKED FRIES

1. Make a big bowl of ice water. Set aside.

2. Peel the potatoes and cut them, lengthwise, into traditional French fries. As you cut, put the potatoes into the ice water.

3. When all of the potatoes have been cut, let them sit in the ice water for 20 minutes.

4. Preheat the oven to 450°F.

5. Remove the potatoes from the water and pat very dry with paper towel. They must be completely dry.

6. Place the potatoes on a rimmed, nonstick baking pan. Add the oil, chili powder, salt, and pepper and toss to coat. Spread the potatoes out in a single layer and place in the preheated oven. Bake, turning occasionally, for about 30 minutes or until the potatoes are cooked through and golden brown.

7. Using a slotted spatula, remove the potatoes to a double layer of paper towel to drain.

8. For extra zip, serve with my special ketchup mix—1 cup sugar-free ketchup, 3 tablespoons LaBelle Hot Flash Hot Sauce, 1 tablespoon prepared horseradish, 1 teaspoon lemon juice.

½ cup nonfat sour cream

½ cup "lite" mayonnaise

Juice and zest of 1 lime

Juice and zest of 1 lemon

2 teaspoons curry powder

1½ pounds cooked medium shrimp, peeled and deveined

2 large ribs celery, well-washed, peeled, and cut, crosswise, into thin slices

1 medium cucumber, peeled, seeded, and thinly sliced

2 tablespoons minced onion

1 teaspoon minced garlic

Salt and white pepper to taste

6 to 8 cups mixed salad greens, well-washed and dried

*T*his very citrusy dressing seems much richer than it actually is. In my opinion, reduced-fat sour cream is one of the best "healthy" products on the market. It still has a creamy texture and great flavor, which adds a lot of character to dressings and sauces.

You can make this salad with cooked chicken, turkey breast or pork tenderloin.

SERVES 6 TO 8

SHRIMP & CELERY SALAD

1. Combine the sour cream, mayonnaise, lime and lemon juice and zest, and curry powder in a medium mixing bowl, whisking to blend well. Add the shrimp along with the celery, cucumber, onion, and garlic. Toss to lightly coat the shrimp and vegetables with the dressing. Season with salt and pepper to taste.

2. Place the greens down the center of a serving platter. Mound the salad on top. Sprinkle with parsley and serve.

This is an easy salad to put together when you have a well-stocked pantry. It keeps well, so it's good to have on hand for spur-of-the-moment dinners. As a variation to the recipe, you can add some diced red bell pepper and change the beans to any you prefer.

SERVES 6

2 cups canned red kidney beans, well-drained

2 cups cooked, sliced green or wax beans

2 cups canned chickpeas (garbanzo beans), well-drained

1 cup finely diced red onion

1 tablespoon LaBelle Sweet Hot Jalapeño Relish

2 teaspoons honey or German sweet mustard

½ cup cider vinegar

Salt and pepper to taste

1 tablespoon chopped parsley

THREE BEAN SALAD

1. Combine the beans, chickpeas, onion, relish, mustard, and vinegar in a serving bowl, tossing and turning to evenly coat. Season with salt and pepper to taste. Set aside to marinate for at least 30 minutes before serving. If marinating for a longer period, cover and refrigerate until ready to serve. The salad can be stored in this fashion for up to 1 week.

2. When ready to serve, stir in the parsley.

1 cup all-purpose flour

1 cup yellow cornmeal

3 tablespoons sugar or sugar
    replacement

2 teaspoons baking powder

1 teaspoon baking soda

½ teaspoon salt

2 cups nonfat buttermilk

2 large eggs (or the equivalent egg
    replacement)

3 tablespoons corn oil or melted
    butter

I love my cornbread. Really, I mean I *love* my cornbread. But, because it's unhealthy to have too often when it's oozing with butter and honey, I devised a healthier version that's just as satisfying. For added zest, you can add finely diced chiles, canned diced green chiles, or finely diced red and green bell peppers to the basic recipe.

MAKES ONE 8-INCH
SQUARE BREAD

As Good As It Gets
Cornbread

1. Preheat the oven to 375°F.

2. Lightly spray the interior of an 8-inch square baking pan or well-seasoned cast-iron skillet with nonstick vegetable spray.

3. Combine the flour, cornmeal, sugar (or sugar replacement), baking powder, baking soda, and salt in a mixing bowl, stirring to blend. Add the buttermilk, eggs (or egg replacement), and oil, stirring to just combine.

4. Scrape into the prepared pan and place in the preheated oven. Bake for about 25 minutes or until the top is golden and a cake tester inserted into the center comes out clean.

5. Remove from the oven and let stand for 10 minutes before cutting into squares and serving.

You need a nice, ripe and juicy watermelon to make this drink. It takes a bit of time to strain the juice, but the end result is worth the effort. It's so refreshing and works well for a crowd. It tastes just as good with or without the alcohol, so kids can drink their fill.

MAKES ABOUT 1 GALLON

One 10 pound watermelon

Juice of 4 limes

Juice of 2 lemons

Juice of 2 oranges

1 cup sugar or sugar replacement

1 cup fresh mint leaves

3 cups white rum

½ cup orange liqueur

Mint sprigs for garnish

WATERMELON COOLER

1. Cut the watermelon into chunks. Remove and discard the seeds. Working in batches, purée the watermelon in the bowl of a food processor fitted with the metal blade.

2. When all of the watermelon has been puréed, strain the purée through a fine mesh sieve into a large, clean container—a gallon jug is great. This will take a bit of time, because you want to strain out all of the juice.

3. Stir the lime, lemon, and orange juices, sugar (or sugar replacement), and mint into the juice along with 6 cups of water, stirring to combine.

4. Refrigerate for a couple of hours or until very cold.

5. You can either serve the cooler plain or add the alcohol. Serve over chopped ice, garnished with a mint sprig.

Smack Yo' Mama Seafood

*S*ome time ago I was in Philadelphia participating in a choir challenge and there was a group of fans outside having a "Patti attack." They desperately wanted to meet me, so I asked the producers to let them in. One of the ladies was so excited that she was on the verge of tears. I was about to give her a hug to comfort her, and I stopped in my tracks—I smelled something very familiar.

"Have you been frying fish?" I asked her.

"Yes, I have." She looked a little embarrassed.

"What kind?" I wanted to know.

"*Porgies!*" she squealed.

Everyone fell out laughing. I explained to them that the smell brought back so many special memories. As a little girl my parents would have parties every weekend and my mother would make fried fish dinners that you could smell from blocks away. She could sure throw down—frying porgies, whiting, and croaker. You can't just go into an upscale supermarket and buy that. Sure, you can get salmon, flounder, tilapia and the like—but you can't get porgies. So, my mother did all of the heavy cooking at the weekend parties, and my father would make the potato salad and other side dishes. It was a neighborhood feast. I remember that my dad also sold liquor along with the food—at $5 a plate, my parents would rack up some big bucks with their fried fish, potato salad and collard greens dinners.

Smelling that smell brought back all of those wonderful memories. So much so, that I had a craving for porgies. I had to get some. The next day, I was in Harlem for an event and the people running it asked me if they could get me anything. I said, "Yes! Some fried porgies!" I don't know where they went, but they brought back some of the best fried porgies in Harlem—but they still didn't top my mother's porgies.

Over the years I have developed dozens of recipes for some wonderful seafood dishes, but nothing compares to Mama's Fried Porgies—and I share my secret recipe for this special childhood dish in this chapter!

MAMA'S FRIED PORGIES

BLACKENED GRILLED HALIBUT

GRILLED TUNA WITH WASABI HOLLANDAISE

MY HOUSE TUNA MELTS

SALMON WITH LEMON-CHILE BUTTER

HONEY-MUSTARD SALMON

BARBECUED SALMON

SALMON BURGERS

DEEP DISH CRAB BAKE

SWEET AND SPICY SHRIMP

BAKED SEAFOOD SURPRISE

POACHED SALMON WITH
BASIL CREAM SAUCE AND FETTUCCINE

SIMPLE SHRIMP LINGUINE

TOMATOES STUFFED WITH SHRIMP SALAD

SHRIMP CAESAR SALAD

Six 6- to 8-ounce porgies, scaled, cleaned,
head and tail removed, and split in half,
lengthwise

Seasoned salt and ground black pepper to taste

1 cup cornmeal

1 cup all-purpose flour

1 teaspoon paprika

½ teaspoon cayenne pepper

½ cup low-fat evaporated milk

Approximately 4 cups "lite" olive oil for frying

Your favorite LaBelle hot sauce for serving

Lemon wedges for serving

*W*hen I was a girl, my mother used lard to fry her fish. Now, I know I'm deviating from the original formula, but I like to use "lite" olive oil instead—it's healthier and still has a great flavor. You can use this recipe to fry almost any type of fish. Try it!

SERVES 6

MAMA'S FRIED PORGIES

1. Rinse the fish under cold, running water and pat dry. Season with seasoned salt and pepper to taste.

2. Place the cornmeal and flour in a large shallow dish. Stir in the paprika, cayenne, and salt and pepper to taste.

3. Dip the seasoned porgies into the milk and then roll them in the seasoned cornmeal.

4. Heat the oil in a large, deep frying pan over medium-high heat. When almost smoking, add the cornmeal-coated fish. Fry, turning twice, for about 8 minutes or until the fish is golden brown and crispy.

5. Carefully transfer the fish to a double layer of paper towel to drain.

6. Serve hot with your favorite LaBelle hot sauce and lemon wedges.

This is one of my most favorite "just in off of the road" home-cooked meals. It's quick, it's easy and it's satisfying. Plus, it's light and healthy, so it will keep you on the right track.

SERVES 6

Six 6-ounce halibut

1 tablespoon LaBelle Seasoned Pepper Blend or your favorite LaBelle blended seasoning to taste

Salt and ground black pepper to taste

BLACKENED GRILLED HALIBUT

1. Oil the grill and preheat on high.

2. Season both sides of the fish with the blackening spice and salt and pepper to taste.

3. Place on the preheated grill and grill, turning once, for about 8 minutes or until nicely marked by the grill and just barely cooked.

4. Remove from the grill and serve on top of a simple green salad.

½ cup sake

½ cup "lite" soy sauce

2 tablespoons canola oil

½ teaspoon LaBelle Hot Flash Hot
Sauce, plus more to taste

Six 7-ounce, 1-inch-thick tuna steaks

Salt and pepper to taste

3 large very fresh egg yolks, at room
temperature

1 tablespoon fresh lemon juice

1 teaspoon wasabi powder dissolved
in 1 teaspoon water

½ cup warm melted butter

¼ cup pickled ginger

*G*irlfriend goes Asian here! I love the heat from the little green mound of wasabi on a sushi plate. I took it right into my soulful kitchen and devised this dinner party recipe to add zest to a rich, fatty piece of tuna, giving the sushi experience to all those folks who won't eat raw fish.

SERVES 6

GRILLED TUNA WITH WASABI HOLLANDAISE

1. Oil and preheat the grill.

2. Combine the sake, soy sauce, canola oil, and ½ teaspoon of the hot sauce. Rub the mixture into both sides of the tuna.

3. Season the tuna with salt and pepper to taste and place on the preheated grill. Grill, turning occasionally, for about 6 minutes for medium-rare.

4. While the tuna is grilling, make the sauce. Place the egg yolks, lemon juice, wasabi powder and salt and hot sauce to taste in the blender jar. Process on high for 1 minute. With the motor running, add the butter in a steady stream. It should take about another 30 seconds or so for the sauce to thicken. Watch very carefully because if you overprocess, the sauce will break. (If necessary, transfer the blender jar to a bowl of very warm water to keep the sauce warm until ready to use. Do not use boiling or very hot water or the sauce will cook.)

5. Place the tuna on a serving platter, drizzle with the sauce, and garnish with pickled ginger.

1 cup chopped black olives

½ cup roasted red peppers

1 tablespoon garlic

1 tablespoon chopped basil leaves

2 tablespoons olive oil

1 teaspoon lemon juice

Six 4-ounce tuna steaks

1 tablespoon vegetable oil

Salt and pepper to taste

Six large slices Italian bread, toasted

12 slices Monterey pepper jack cheese

I love diner food, but once in a while I like to take the standard dishes to new places. My version of an old-fashioned tuna melt is about as good as it gets. This is also a great way to make a grilled chicken sandwich. It's a perfect Sunday, television-watching dinner sandwich—so serve it with some salad and a cool drink, turn on the tube, and enjoy!

SERVES 6

MY HOUSE TUNA MELTS

1. Combine the olives, peppers, garlic and basil in the bowl of a food processor fitted with the metal blade, processing to just blend. Add the olive oil and lemon juice and, using quick on and off turns, process to a chunky purée.

2. Preheat the broiler.

3. Lightly coat the tuna with oil and season with salt and pepper to taste. Place the tuna on a nonstick grill pan over medium-high heat and grill, turning occasionally, for about 5 minutes or until the tuna is medium rare.

4. Slather a good layer of the olive mixture on each piece of toast. Place a tuna steak on top and cover each one with 2 pieces of cheese.

5. Place under the broiler and broil for about 45 seconds or just until the cheese has melted and is lightly colored.

6. Serve immediately while the cheese is still melting.

*S*almon has become such an everyday kind of fish that I'm always trying to think of new ways to cook it. I devised this one when I had some company coming and wanted to cook light, but fun. I think that the fresh herb and lemon coating does the trick. If, like me, you like it hot, add some of my hot sauce to the coating for the salmon.

SERVES 6

¼ cup chopped onion

1 tablespoon chopped garlic

1 tablespoon chopped parsley

1 tablespoon lemon zest

1½ teaspoons paprika

1 teaspoon ground white pepper

1 teaspoon chopped fresh dill

½ cup butter

1 tablespoon crushed red pepper flakes

¼ cup fresh lemon juice

Six 7-ounce salmon steaks or fillets

Salt to taste

SALMON WITH LEMON-CHILE BUTTER

1. Combine the onion, garlic and parsley with 2 teaspoons of the lemon zest and the paprika, pepper and dill in the small bowl of a food processor fitted with the metal blade. Process to a thick purée. Cover and refrigerate until ready to use.

2. Place the butter in a small saucepan over low heat and heat until melted. Add the red pepper flakes and let stand for 1 hour, keeping the butter warm. When infused with the pepper, strain into a small frying pan, taking care to leave the milky solids in the bottom of the pan. Discard the pepper flakes.

(continued)

3. Preheat the broiler.

4. Place the butter over medium heat and cook, stirring occasionally, until the butter begins to smell nutty and is golden brown. Remove from the heat and stir in 1 tablespoon of the lemon juice and 1 teaspoon of the zest. Keep warm while you cook the salmon.

5. Rub both sides of the salmon with lemon juice. Place half of the onion mixture on one side of each piece of salmon, pressing it down to adhere. Place the salmon on a broiler pan under the preheated broiler, coated side up, and broil for 4 minutes. Carefully turn and coat the remaining side and broil it for an additional 4 minutes or until just barely cooked through.

6. Remove from the broiler and serve drizzled with the butter.

he spicy mustard and sweet honey are the perfect combination to add zest to salmon. This method of preparation also works well for grilled pork or chicken.

SERVES 6

¾ cup honey

¾ cup Dijon mustard

1½ teaspoons paprika

1 teaspoon dried basil

¾ teaspoon dried parsley flakes

Six 8-ounce salmon fillets or steaks

Salt and ground black pepper to taste

HONEY-MUSTARD SALMON

1. Preheat the oven to 350°F.

2. Lightly coat the interior of a 9-inch × 13-inch baking dish with vegetable oil. Set aside.

3. Combine the honey, mustard, paprika, basil and parsley in a small mixing bowl, whisking to blend completely.

4. Season the salmon with salt and pepper to taste. Place the fish in the prepared baking dish and, using a pastry brush, generously coat the fish with half of the honey-mustard mixture.

5. Place in the preheated oven and bake for 20 minutes.

6. Brush the remaining honey-mustard mixture on the fish and continue to bake for an additional 5 minutes.

7. Remove from the oven and serve.

2 tablespoons vegetable oil

1 cup finely minced onion

1 tablespoon finely minced garlic

3 cups ketchup

1 cup beer

6 tablespoons light brown sugar

½ cup cider vinegar

3 tablespoons Worcestershire
    sauce

1½ tablespoons chili powder

1 tablespoon LaBelle Rich Red
    Hot Sauce

2 teaspoons dry mustard

Six 6-ounce skinless salmon
    fillets

Salt to taste

Ground black pepper to taste

*C*ooking the salmon in aluminum foil allows the barbecue sauce to really penetrate the fish while also keeping the salmon very moist. This sauce goes well with almost any meat or fish, so make sure to save any that remains. It will keep in the fridge for a month or so. I like to make a big batch (this recipe makes a quart) and keep it on hand for a spur-of-the-moment indoor or outdoor barbecue.

If you like, you can unwrap the salmon and place it under the broiler for a minute or two to get a nice glaze going.

SERVES 6

BARBECUED SALMON

1. Heat the oil in a medium saucepan over medium heat. Add the onion and garlic and sauté for 4 minutes or until beginning to color. Stir in the ketchup, beer, brown sugar, vinegar, Worcestershire sauce, chili powder, Hot Flash and mustard. Bring to a simmer; then, lower the heat and cook, stirring frequently, at a bare simmer for 20 minutes or until the flavors have blended and the sauce is thick.

2. Remove from the heat and set aside to cool.

3. Season the salmon with salt and pepper to taste. Place the fish in a large resealable bag. Add just enough sauce to lightly coat the fish. Seal and press on the bag to evenly coat. Refrigerate for 1 hour.

4. Preheat the oven to 350°F.

5. Cut six pieces of heavy-duty aluminum foil large enough to completely wrap a piece of salmon.

6. Remove the salmon from the plastic bag and place a fillet in the center of each piece of foil. Then, wrap the foil around the salmon to tightly seal. Place the salmon packets on a baking dish in the preheated oven and bake for 10 minutes or just until the salmon is barely cooked in the center.

7. Remove from the oven and carefully open the foil to release some of the steam.

8. Brush each piece of salmon with some of the remaining sauce and serve.

Three 8-ounce cans salmon, well-
    drained with juice reserved,
    bones removed and discarded

2 tablespoons butter

1 small onion, peeled and
    minced

½ cup minced red bell pepper

1 large egg

¾ cup breadcrumbs, plain or
    Italian-flavored

¼ cup mayonnaise

1 tablespoon chopped parsley

1 teaspoon Dijon mustard

¼ teaspoon LaBelle Rich Red
    Hot Sauce

¼ teaspoon lemon juice

Seasoned salt and ground black
    pepper to taste

3 tablespoons vegetable oil

6 potato rolls, split and toasted

Cole slaw, optional

I grew up on canned salmon cakes. I've updated the old-fashioned salmon croquette a bit with my version of salmon burgers. You can make them with fresh salmon, but since I always have canned salmon in the pantry for a quick salad, it's just more convenient to use it for burgers. Don't be afraid to glaze them with some barbecue sauce for even more of a traditional burger flavor.

SERVES 6

SALMON BURGERS

1. Place the salmon in a medium mixing bowl. Set aside.

2. Heat the butter in a medium frying pan over medium heat. Add the onion and bell pepper and sauté for about 2 minutes or just until soft. Remove from the heat and let cool slightly.

3. Scrape the onion/bell pepper mixture into the salmon. Add the egg, breadcrumbs, mayonnaise, parsley, and mustard. Using your hands, mix well to combine. If the mixture seems a bit dry, add a bit more mayonnaise; if too wet, a little more breadcrumbs. Season with hot sauce, lemon juice, and salt and pepper to taste.

4. Form the salmon mixture into six patties of equal size.

5. Return the frying pan to medium heat and add the oil. When hot, add the salmon patties and fry for about 4 minutes per side or until golden brown and hot in the center.

6. Remove from the oven and carefully transfer a patty to each of the buns. Serve immediately, topped with cole slaw (see page 148) or the fixin's of your choice.

3 tablespoons butter

1½ tablespoons all-purpose flour

1½ cups half-and-half

2 tablespoons sherry wine

1 tablespoon Old Bay seasoning

1 teaspoon onion powder

1 teaspoon garlic powder

Salt and ground black pepper to taste

2 pounds backfin crabmeat, shell and
cartilage removed

1 teaspoon paprika

This is a classic Maryland crab dish that is great for lunch or late supper. I sometimes make a batch early in the day and then pop it into the oven after a show. It tastes just as good reheated as it does fresh. Of course, hot sauce makes the flavor of this dish really pop, so pour it on.

SERVES 6

DEEP DISH CRAB BAKE

1. Preheat the oven to 350°F.

2. Lightly oil a 2-quart casserole. Set aside.

3. Heat the butter in a medium saucepan over medium heat. Add the flour, stirring to blend well, and cook for 2 minutes. Whisking constantly, slowly add the half-and-half and cook, stirring frequently, for about 4 minutes or until thickened and the starchy taste has cooked out.

4. Whisk in the sherry, Old Bay, onion powder, and garlic powder along with salt and pepper to taste. Cook for just a minute or two to allow flavors to blend.

5. Place the crab in the bottom of the prepared casserole. Pour the sauce over the top, stirring to just combine.

6. Sprinkle the paprika over the top and place in the preheated oven. Bake for 20 minutes or until the top is golden brown and the sauce is bubbling.

7. Remove from the oven and serve, piping hot.

One 6-ounce can pineapple juice

½ cup "lite" soy sauce

1½ tablespoons sesame oil

2 teaspoons sugar or the equivalent amount of sugar substitute

2 teaspoons LaBelle Hot Flash Hot Sauce, or to taste

2 teaspoons cornstarch

1 large onion, peeled and cut, lengthwise, into thin strips

1 large green bell pepper, well-washed, cored, seeded, membrane removed, and cut, lengthwise, into thin strips

1 large carrot, peeled, trimmed, and cut, crosswise on the diagonal, into thin slices

1½ pounds medium shrimp, peeled, deveined, and tails removed

1 tablespoon fresh lemon juice

¼ cup chopped scallions with some green part, optional

Who needs Chinese take-out when you've got Miss Patti? Cook up a pot of rice, put the chopsticks on the table, and you don't have to wait for the doorbell to ring. Add a bottle of crisp white wine or some Asian beer and the party can start.

SERVES 6

SWEET AND SPICY SHRIMP

1. Combine the pineapple juice and soy sauce with the ½ teaspoon of the sesame oil and the sugar and hot sauce in a small saucepan. Stir in the cornstarch and place over medium heat. Bring to a simmer and then lower the heat and simmer for about 3 minutes or until thickened slightly. Remove from the heat and set aside.

2. Heat the remaining sesame oil in a wok over high heat. When almost smoking, add the onion, bell pepper, and carrot and cook, stirring and tossing, for about 3 minutes or until the vegetables are crisp-tender.

3. Season the shrimp with the lemon juice and add to the vegetables, stirring and tossing to just combine.

4. Add the reserved soy sauce mixture and cook, stirring and tossing, for about 3 minutes or until the shrimp is cooked through and the sauce has thickened.

5. Remove from the heat and serve, garnished with scallions, if desired.

5 tablespoons "lite" olive oil

1 red bell pepper, well-washed, cored, seeded, membrane removed, and chopped

1 green bell pepper, well-washed, cored, seeded, membrane removed, and chopped

1 cup finely chopped onions

2 teaspoons minced garlic

1½ cups diced seeded plum tomatoes

½ cup dry white wine

1 teaspoon dried oregano

⅛ teaspoon crushed red pepper flakes

LaBelle Seasoned Sea Salt and Seasoned Pepper to taste

1 pound sea scallops

1 pound large shrimp, tails removed, peeled, and deveined

½ pound lump crabmeat, any shell and cartilage removed

½ cup crumbled feta cheese

1 teaspoon chopped flat leaf parsley

*Y*ou can have this dish ready and waiting in the fridge. The doorbell rings, throw it in the oven, and—surprise!—dinner is served. This is my take on the wonderful Greek recipes that perfectly blend oregano, plum tomatoes and sharp feta cheese into aromatic and refreshing dishes.

SERVES 6

BAKED SEAFOOD SURPRISE

124

1. Preheat the oven to 400°F.

2. Using 3 tablespoons of the olive oil, generously coat the interior of a 9-inch × 13-inch baking dish.

3. Heat the remaining 2 tablespoons of olive oil in a large frying pan over medium-high heat. Add the red and green peppers, onions, and garlic and cook, stirring frequently, for about 4 minutes or just until wilted.

4. Add the tomatoes, wine, oregano, red pepper flakes along with salt and pepper to taste. (Remember, you are going to add some feta cheese, which is salty, so go easy on the salt here.) Bring to a boil, lower the heat, and simmer for 5 minutes.

5. Place the scallops, shrimp, and crabmeat in an even layer in the bottom of the prepared baking dish. Pour the tomato mixture over the top, sprinkle with feta cheese, and place in the preheated oven.

6. Bake for about 12 minutes or until the seafood is cooked, the cheese is golden, and the sauce is bubbling.

7. Remove from the oven, sprinkle with parsley, and serve.

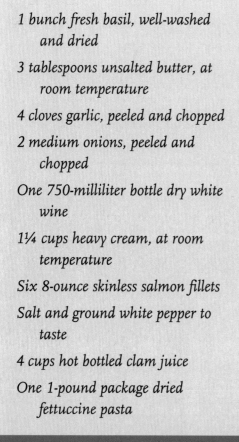

1 bunch fresh basil, well-washed
  and dried

3 tablespoons unsalted butter, at
  room temperature

4 cloves garlic, peeled and chopped

2 medium onions, peeled and
  chopped

One 750-milliliter bottle dry white
  wine

1¼ cups heavy cream, at room
  temperature

Six 8-ounce skinless salmon fillets

Salt and ground white pepper to
  taste

4 cups hot bottled clam juice

One 1-pound package dried
  fettuccine pasta

*T*his is a very elegant pasta dish. The cream sauce just lifts the salmon right up and makes it extraordinary. It is one of my favorite recipes for entertaining my girlfriends at lunchtime. If you are doing some real fancy entertaining, reduce the salmon to a 4-ounce piece, lessen the pasta, and serve it as a first course.

SERVES 6

POACHED SALMON WITH BASIL CREAM SAUCE AND FETTUCCINE

1. Remove the basil leaves from the stems. Cut the basil leaves into thin strips and set aside. Separately reserve the stems.

2. Heat the butter in a large nonreactive saucepan over medium-high heat. Add the garlic and onions and cook, stirring, for about 2 minutes or just until the garlic is lightly colored. Add the wine and bring to a boil. Lower

the heat and simmer for about 15 minutes or until the liquid has reduced by half. Remove from the heat and strain through a fine mesh sieve, discarding the garlic and onions. Return the liquid to the saucepan.

3. While the wine is reducing, combine the cream and basil stems in a small saucepan over medium heat. Bring to a simmer and simmer for about 10 minutes or until the cream is well-infused with the basil and reduced to 1 cup. Remove from the heat and strain through a fine mesh sieve, discarding the basil stems. Pour the reduced cream into the saucepan with the wine.

4. Return the liquid to medium heat and bring to a boil. Lower the heat and simmer for about 10 minutes or until quite thick. Season with salt and pepper to taste.

5. While the sauce is reducing, poach the salmon.

6. Place the clam juice in a large sauté pan over medium-high heat. Bring to a simmer. Add the salmon, cover, and cook at a bare simmer for about 10 minutes or until the salmon is just barely cooked through.

7. Using a slotted spatula, transfer the salmon to a serving platter and tent lightly with aluminum foil to keep warm.

8. Measure out ¼ cup of the poaching liquid and set aside.

9. While the sauce is reducing and salmon is poaching, cook the pasta to "al dente" according to package directions. Drain well and return to the cooking pot. Add the remaining tablespoon of butter along with the ¼ cup of poaching liquid. Season with salt and pepper to taste along with half of the basil leaves. Stir to just moisten.

10. Using tongs, place an equal portion of the pasta in the center of each of 6 large, shallow soup bowls. Place a piece of salmon in the center of the pasta and spoon an equal portion of the remaining sauce over the fish in each bowl. Sprinkle with the remaining basil leaves and serve.

1 cup olive oil

6 cloves garlic, peeled and slivered

1 medium onion, peeled and chopped

½ tablespoon crushed red pepper flakes

1 cup diced tomatoes (canned is fine)

Salt and pepper to taste

1½ pounds fresh linguine, cooked according to package directions

1½ pounds cooked medium shrimp, tails removed, peeled, and deveined

¼ cup butter, at room temperature

1 tablespoon chopped fresh parsley

A trip to Philadelphia's Italian neighborhood was my inspiration for this dish. It's elegant, but easy. I like to serve it family-style on a platter in the center of the table with a big green salad and lots of hot garlic bread. If you want to step it up, just add scallops, crabmeat, or clams and mussels.

SERVES 6

SIMPLE SHRIMP LINGUINE

1. Combine the oil with the garlic, onion and red pepper flakes in a small saucepan over high heat. Cook, stirring occasionally for about 4 minutes or until very fragrant.

2. Add the tomatoes, stirring to combine. Season with salt and pepper, remove from the heat, and set aside.

3. Cook the pasta in boiling salted water according to the package directions for "al dente." About a minute before the pasta is ready, add the shrimp to just heat it through. Drain well, reserving 1 cup of the pasta cooking water.

4. Return the pasta to the saucepan, add the butter along with just enough of the reserved cooking water to moisten. Season with salt and pepper to taste and stir to combine.

5. Pour the reserved oil mixture over the pasta and toss to combine. If the mixture seems too dry, add a bit more of the reserved pasta water.

6. Using tongs, transfer the pasta to a serving platter. Sprinkle with parsley and serve.

6 large ripe tomatoes

1 ripe avocado

1 teaspoon fresh lime juice

1 pound cooked small shrimp,
  peeled, deveined, and tails
  removed

½ cup "lite" mayonnaise

2 tablespoons minced scallion
  with some green part

1 tablespoon minced pickled
  (sushi) ginger

Salt and pepper to taste

Fresh parsley or cilantro sprigs
  for garnish

12 small pretty lettuce leaves

*W*hen my girlfriends gather for lunch, this is the most requested dish. I've done it for every type of get-together. It's easy, delicious, light and looks pretty on the plate. If you want a bit of zest, add some LaBelle Pepper Clear Mild Pepper Sauce to the salad. If you want to fancy it up even more, make a little avocado salsa to top it off—just dice some ripe avocado, add some minced onion and cilantro, season with lime juice, hot sauce, and you've got it!

SERVES 6

TOMATOES STUFFED WITH SHRIMP SALAD

1. Cut the top quarter off of each tomato. Scoop out the seeds and pulp and place the tomatoes, cut side down, on a double layer of paper towel to drain for at least 15 minutes.

2. Peel and seed the avocado. Chop the flesh and place it in a shallow bowl, add the lime juice, and, using a kitchen fork, mash until quite smooth.

3. Place the shrimp in a medium mixing bowl. Add the avocado along with the mayonnaise, scallions, and ginger. Season with salt and pepper and gently toss to completely blend. Stuff an equal portion of the salad into each tomato, mounding it slightly. Garnish with a sprig of parsley or cilantro

4. Place a couple of nice lettuce leaves on each of six plates. Place a tomato in the center and serve.

LaBelle Seasoned Sea Salt

1 clove garlic, peeled

2 medium heads romaine
    lettuce, washed, trimmed,
    well-dried, and torn into
    bite-sized pieces

24 warm grilled shrimp

6 anchovy fillets, very well-
    drained and finely
    chopped

1 soft-boiled large egg, chopped

1 cup large croutons

½ cup olive oil

¼ cup grated Parmesan
    cheese

1 tablespoon fresh lemon juice

Don't you just love a big, crisp Caesar salad? I do, and I think mine, with some tasty shrimp on top, is the best. I love to toss it at the table, just to put on a little show! I always serve this salad with lots of crusty garlic bread and some chilled white wine. I use my stovetop grill pan to quickly grill the shrimp, but you can use any type of cooked shrimp.

In a pinch, just buy a good quality, refrigerated Caesar dressing, but still put the salad together at the table—just for the drama.

SERVES 6

SHRIMP CAESAR SALAD

1. Sprinkle salt into a wooden salad bowl. Using the garlic clove, rub the salt into the bowl so that it is seasoned with garlic. Place the bowl on a serving tray. Add the lettuce to the bowl.

2. Place the shrimp, anchovies, chopped egg, olive oil, croutons, cheese, and lemon juice in bowls on the serving tray.

3. Place the dressing in a sauceboat and bring the tray and sauceboat to the table.

4. Pour the dressing over the lettuce, tossing to evenly coat. Add the eggs, croutons, cheese, and lemon juice to the salad, again tossing to evenly distribute.

5. Either place the shrimp on top of the salad in the large bowl and garnish with the anchovies or individually plate the salad and place 4 shrimp and 1 anchovy fillet on top of each one.

CAESAR DRESSING

1. Combine the egg yolk with the lemon juice, vinegar, and mustard powder in a small nonreactive mixing bowl. Using a handheld electric mixer, beat until well-blended. With the motor running, slowly add the oil, beating until well emulsified.

2. Fold in the anchovies, cheese and capers. Season with white pepper and serve.

1 large egg yolk, beaten

¼ cup fresh lemon juice

3 tablespoons white wine vinegar

1½ tablespoons dry mustard powder

1 cup "lite" olive oil

3 anchovy fillets, well-drained and chopped

¼ cup grated Parmesan cheese

1 tablespoon minced capers

Freshly ground white pepper to taste

Celebrate!

In this chapter, I decided to do something a little different and give you some menu ideas to prepare for your next backyard barbecue, brunch or holiday feast. A good meal is just food when eaten alone, but when served to people you love, it becomes an event!

Family and friends are the foundation for a successful gathering. The food, like glue, can just bring everything together and make it worth it. The inspiration for all of my recipes is the people I love. I imagine the smiles on their faces when they take that first bite of potato salad or lick the BBQ sauce off of their fingers from my melt-in-your-mouth ribs.

Like I've said, it's not just about the food. One of my favorite ways to entertain is to host a brunch. Brunch allows you to have so much more freedom in your meals. You can have breakfast dishes, like my egg white and cheese omelet. Or, you can have lunch staples, like my sweet and savory grilled cheese sandwich. You can even throw in a heavy dinner meal, like my brown sugar baked country ham. Add a couple of good friends to go along with the good food, and you can't go wrong.

I also love cookouts and barbecues. It's so rewarding to see the family really let loose, come together, and kick back in the yard. This is where I break out the standards—my famous hot 'n' spicy potato salad and my tender and juicy baby back ribs. Those two dishes alone get people singing my praises. And if you follow my recipes, they'll be singing your praises, too!

Bangin' Barbecues

JUST LIKE I LIKE IT FRIED CHICKEN

TENDER AND JUICY BARBECUED
BABY BACK RIBS

BARBECUED SHRIMP

MEATY BAKED BEANS

GRILLED CORN ON THE COB
WITH CHILE-BUTTER

MY FAMOUS HOT AND SPICY POTATO SALAD

CREAMY AND NUTTY COLE SLAW

MISS PATTI'S PICKLES

LIP SMACKIN' PINK LEMONADE

SWEET TEA WITH LEMON AND LIME

Two 3-pound frying chickens, cut into serving pieces, rinsed, and patted dry

1 tablespoon LaBelle Seasoned Sea Salt, or to taste

1 tablespoon cayenne pepper

1 tablespoon paprika

LaBelle Seasoned Pepper

1½ cups all-purpose flour

Salt and black pepper, optional

About 6 cups vegetable oil, for frying

*W*ho doesn't love fried chicken? Sure, maybe we shouldn't eat it every day, but it's worth an off-the-diet splurge once in a while. I like my chicken fried up very hot and spicy. If you are not into heat, just season with the paprika and leave all of the hot sauce on the table for me!

SERVES 6

JUST LIKE I LIKE IT FRIED CHICKEN

1. Line a baking sheet with two layers of paper towel. Generously season the chicken pieces with seasoning salt, cayenne, paprika, and seasoning pepper to taste.

2. Place the flour on a plate and, if desired, season it with salt and pepper to taste. Roll each piece of chicken in it to lightly coat.

3. Pour about ¾ inch of oil into a large deep skillet. Heat over high heat until the oil reaches 365°F on a candy thermometer. Working in batches, add the chicken pieces to the oil. (Don't crowd the skillet, or the chicken won't be crispy.)

4. Cover the pan and fry, turning once, for about 20 minutes or until the chicken is cooked through, crisp, and golden brown. You'll need to control the heat (reduce to medium-high, then back again) throughout the cooking time to maintain the oil temperature and keep the chicken from getting too dark before it is cooked through.

5. Carefully remove the chicken from the pan and drain on paper towels. Repeat with remaining chicken, adding oil to the skillet as necessary (remember to bring it to temperature before adding chicken).

6. Serve fried chicken hot, warm or at room temperature. You know me— I suggest serving it hot!

Two 1½- to 2-pound racks
  baby back ribs

3 tablespoons LaBelle Seasoned
  Pepper Blend or your
  favorite LaBelle blended
  seasoning to taste

1 cup ketchup

¼ cup molasses

2 tablespoons light brown sugar

2 tablespoons Worcestershire
  sauce

2 tablespoons liquid smoke

1 teaspoon "lite" soy sauce

½ teaspoon LaBelle Hot Flash
  Hot Sauce

*T*he great thing about these ribs is that in a couple of hours you'll have the tenderest, juiciest, backyard-barbecue–tasting ribs you've ever had—with almost no work! If it's grilling season, use the outdoor grill. If not, the oven works almost as well (and if you use disposable pans, the cleanup will be a breeze). Take my advice—double or triple the recipe, because this one is popular and goes fast!

If you know company is coming, bake the ribs a day in advance and marinate in the fridge overnight—the extra marinating time will give them a deep, rich smoky flavor.

SERVES 6

TENDER AND JUICY BARBECUED BABY BACK RIBS

1. Preheat the oven to 300°F.

2. Generously coat both sides of the ribs with the blackening spice. Place on a foil-lined baking sheet, cover with foil, and bake for 1 hour.

3. Combine the ketchup, molasses, brown sugar, Worcestershire sauce, liquid smoke, soy sauce, and hot sauce in a mixing bowl, stirring to blend well. Divide the mixture in half. Use half for basting and set the other half aside. Remove the racks from the oven and liberally coat each rack with some of the ketchup mixture. (If you're making the ribs ahead, cover with foil and refrigerate until you're ready to grill them.)

4. If grilling, oil and preheat the grill.

5. To grill, place the racks on the outside edge of the grill away from direct heat, cover, and grill, turning occasionally and basting with some of the sauce, for 2½ hours or until the meat is very tender and almost falling off the bone.

6. If you like a little more char on your ribs, uncover the grill and raise the temperature to medium-high. Move the racks to direct heat and grill, turning frequently, for 10 minutes.

7. If baking, place the racks in a large, shallow baking pan (or disposable aluminum pan), and cover completely with aluminum foil. Bake in the preheated 300°F oven, turning and basting with some of the sauce, for 2 hours or until the ribs are very tender and the meat is almost falling off the bone.

8. If you like, heat the reserved sauce in a small saucepan over low heat just before the ribs are ready.

9. Remove the ribs from the grill or oven and serve hot with the reserved sauce for dipping.

⅛ cup butter

3 cloves garlic, peeled and minced

3 tablespoons bottled chili sauce

1½ tablespoons Worcestershire sauce

1½ tablespoons orange juice

1½ tablespoons lemon juice

2 teaspoons maple syrup

2 teaspoons chopped parsley

3 pounds jumbo shrimp

3 tablespoons LaBelle Sweet Hot Jalapeño Relish

LaBelle Pepper Clear Mild Pepper Sauce

*Y*ou can barbecue any size shrimp, but I just love the big guys—the colossal ones (10 to a pound) when I can get them, and jumbos (about 15 to a pound) when I can't. The sweet-spicy marinade sticks to the shells and to your fingers—it's a real finger-lickin' kind of dish that's best eaten outside, far away from your nice couch, drapes, linens and anything else that will be stained by sticky fingers.

SERVES 6 TO 8

BARBECUED SHRIMP

1. Combine the butter with the garlic, chili sauce, Worcestershire sauce, orange and lemon juices, maple syrup, and parsley in a small saucepan over medium heat. Heat for about 3 minutes or until the butter has melted.

2. Cut the shrimp down the center back, leaving the shells on. Place the shrimp in a shallow baking pan and pour the butter mixture over the top, add the relish, and toss to coat well. Cover with plastic film and refrigerate for 3 hours.

3. Oil and preheat the grill.

4. Place the marinated shrimp on the grill and grill, turning frequently, for about 5 minutes or until lightly charred and cooked through.

I know it seems like overkill to add beef to pork and beans, but the meatiness turns the beans into a whole new dining experience. This is a recipe that can easily be tripled to feed a crowd for any gathering or event. It's easy to put together, filling and makes a complete meal when served with salad.

SERVES 6

1 pound lean ground beef

Two 8-ounce cans pork and beans

¼ teaspoon dry mustard powder

Light brown sugar

Salt and freshly ground pepper

MEATY BAKED BEANS

1. Preheat the oven to 350°F. Line a baking sheet with a double layer of paper towels. Lightly spray a 2-quart casserole with nonstick vegetable spray. Set aside.

2. Place the ground beef in nonstick frying pan over medium-high heat. Cook, stirring frequently, for about 5 minutes or until the meat has broken into small pieces and is nicely browned.

3. Using a slotted spoon, transfer the beef to the paper towels to drain any excess fat.

4. Combine the drained beef with the beans, mustard, and brown sugar to taste in the prepared casserole, stirring well to blend. Taste and, if necessary, add salt and pepper.

5. Place in the preheated oven and bake for about 45 minutes or until thick and bubbling. Remove from the oven and serve.

143

*T*his is a great way to make corn! You don't have to heat up the kitchen with that big pot of boiling water. I always make two ears for everyone, knowing full well that nobody can eat just one—particularly once they get a taste of my Chile Butter!

SERVES 6

12 ears corn in the husk

Melted butter, for brushing

Chile Butter (recipe follows)

GRILLED CORN ON THE COB WITH CHILE-BUTTER

1. Fold back the husks from each cob (leave them attached) and carefully remove all of the silk. When clean, pull the husks back up and over the corn to enclose them completely.

2. Place the corn in cold water to cover for 1 hour or up to 4 hours. (This can easily be done in a sink or large tub.)

3. Preheat and oil the grill.

4. Remove the corn from the water and drain well.

5. Pull back the husk from each cob and brush the kernels with melted butter. Pull the husks back up and cover the corn to enclose completely.

6. Place on the preheated grill and grill, turning frequently, for 30 minutes or until the husks are charred and the corn is juicy and tender.

7. Remove from the grill, fold back the husks (they're the perfect handles for hot corn) and serve hot with Chile Butter.

CHILE BUTTER

1. Place the butter in a small mixing bowl. Add the cilantro, jalapeños, lemon juice, and cayenne and beat with a wooden spoon for about 3 minutes or until very well blended.

½ cup salted butter, softened

2 tablespoons chopped cilantro

2 tablespoons LaBelle Diced Fine Jalapeños

1 teaspoon fresh lemon juice

½ teaspoon cayenne pepper

2. Using a rubber spatula, scrape the butter onto the edge of a piece of waxed paper. Bring the paper up and over the butter, then roll the butter into a log about 1 inch in diameter (the log should be completely enclosed in the waxed paper). Twist the ends of the paper together.

3. Place in the freezer for about 15 minutes or until quite firm.

4. Unwrap and cut, crosswise, into ¼-inch thick pieces.

5. Place the butter "pats" in a single layer on a sheet of waxed paper. Cover with another sheet of waxed paper and refrigerate until ready to use.

(If all this seems like too much work, just mix it up and scrape the butter into a crock for the table.)

*I*f you like potato salad, you'll love this one—sweet and hot, and perfect for a barbecue or picnic. I particularly like the combination of the crunchy fresh celery and the pungent celery seeds. You can even add a bit more heat—you know I always do! The recipe can easily be doubled or tripled if you have a crowd coming over.

SERVES 6 TO 8

10 cooked red new potatoes, cubed

2 ribs celery, well-washed, trimmed, peeled, and chopped

½ green bell pepper, well-washed, cored, seeded, membrane removed, and chopped

1 cup diced white onion

4 hard-boiled eggs, peeled and chopped

⅛ cup mayonnaise

3 tablespoons LaBelle Diced Fine Jalapeños

2 tablespoons LaBelle Sweet Jalapeño Relish

2 tablespoons cider vinegar

1 tablespoon yellow mustard

½ teaspoon celery seed, or to taste

LaBelle Seasoned Sea Salt and Seasoned Pepper

MY FAMOUS HOT AND SPICY POTATO SALAD

1. Combine the potatoes with the celery, bell pepper, and onion in a mixing bowl, tossing to blend. Stir in the eggs.

2. Combine the mayonnaise with the jalapeños, relish, vinegar, and mustard in a small bowl, stirring to blend.

3. Pour the mayonnaise mixture over the potato mixture. Add celery seed and seasoning salt and pepper to taste. Toss just until mixed. (Do not overmix or the potatoes will get mushy.)

4. Transfer the salad to a serving bowl and serve. Or, if not serving immediately, cover with plastic and refrigerate until ready to serve.

1½ cups mayonnaise

¾ cup half-and-half

Juice of 1 lemon

3 tablespoons sugar

2 tablespoons cider vinegar

1 teaspoon celery seed, or to taste

⅛ teaspoon mustard

Salt and freshly ground pepper

1 large head cabbage, well-washed, cored, and shredded

3 medium carrots, trimmed, peeled, and shredded

1 medium red onion, peeled and thinly shaved

½ cup toasted slivered almonds

I like my cole slaw a little bit on the rich, sweet side with just a little kick. For a little more heat, add a tablespoon of my LaBelle Diced Fine Jalapeños or, for a real jolt, a few splashes of my LaBelle Hot Flash Hot Sauce. If you make the slaw early in the day, wait until just before serving to sprinkle with the almonds so the nuts stay crunchy.

SERVES A CROWD

CREAMY AND NUTTY COLE SLAW

1. Combine the mayonnaise and half-and-half with the lemon juice, sugar, vinegar, mustard, and celery seed in a medium mixing bowl, whisking to blend well. Season with salt and pepper to taste.

2. Place the cabbage in a large serving bowl. Add the carrots and onion and toss to combine. Pour the dressing over the top and, using your hands, toss the vegetables in the dressing until well coated.

3. Using a paper towel, clean the edge of the bowl. Top the slaw with the almonds and serve, or cover with plastic and refrigerate until ready to serve.

2½ pounds Kirby (pickling)
    cucumbers, scrubbed very clean

10 cloves garlic, peeled

6 large sprigs fresh dill

4 dried hot red chiles

2 cups white vinegar

2 cups of cold water

½ cup sugar (or sugar substitute
    to equal)

2 tablespoons kosher salt

*T*hese are so easy to make and so good—perfect to add a bit of crunch to the table. These pickles will keep for a few weeks in the fridge, so they are great to keep on hand all summer long.

MAKES 2 QUARTS

MISS PATTI'S PICKLES

Place the cucumbers, garlic, dill and chiles in a large bowl. Add the vinegar along with 2 cups cold water. Stir in the sugar and salt and set aside for 30 minutes, stirring occasionally. When the sugar and salt have dissolved, pack the pickles in quart jars or any clean container with a lid that will hold them submerged in liquid. Refrigerate for at least 24 hours before serving.

Juice of 3 lemons

Juice of 3 limes

½ to ¾ cup sugar, or to taste

2 teaspoons grenadine syrup

4 cups of ice water

½ cup strawberry purée, strained

Crushed ice, for serving

Fresh mint sprigs for garnish, optional

I absolutely love the combination of lemon-lime with the sweet hint of fresh strawberries. You can make gallons of this lemonade and people will still be asking for more. It's a summer standard in my home, and I know it will be in yours as well once your family tastes it.

MAKES ABOUT I QUART

LIP SMACKIN' PINK LEMONADE

1. Combine the lemon and lime juices in a large pitcher. Add the sugar and grenadine, stirring to blend. Add 4 cups of ice water and stir vigorously until the sugar dissolves.

2. Stir in the strawberry purée.

3. Add about a cup of crushed ice and serve. Garnish each glass with a mint sprig, if desired.

*S*outherners sure do like their sweet tea! I probably make mine a little less sweet than the traditional mix, but I will leave the amount of sugar up to you (of course, feel free to use a sugar substitute). If you drink a lot of sweet tea, I suggest that you make simple syrup and keep it in the fridge—it keeps for a long time and adds instant sweetness to all cold drinks. A good ratio for simple syrup is 1 cup sugar to 1 cup water. Combine in a small saucepan and boil for a couple of minutes to dissolve the sugar. Let cool and store tightly covered in the refrigerator.

MAKES ABOUT 2 QUARTS

6 cups of cold water

3 orange pekoe tea bags

One 1-inch piece fresh ginger, thinly sliced

½ cup sugar or sugar replacement, or to taste

1 lemon, well-washed and thinly sliced, crosswise, seeds removed

1 lime, well-washed and thinly sliced, crosswise, seeds removed

Fresh mint sprigs for garnish, optional

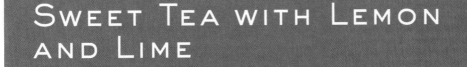

SWEET TEA WITH LEMON AND LIME

1. Place 6 cups cold water in a medium saucepan. Add the tea bags and place over high heat. Bring to a boil; then, immediately remove the pan from the heat. Add the ginger and set aside for 10 minutes to allow the tea to steep.

2. Remove the tea bags and pour the tea into a pitcher. Add the sugar, stirring to dissolve. I usually add ½ cup of sugar or sugar replacement and then add more as needed. Add the lemon and lime slices, stirring to blend. Fill the pitcher with ice and serve, garnished with a mint sprig, if desired.

Beautiful Brunches

EGG WHITE AND CHEESE OMELET

HEARTY BREAKFAST SANDWICHES

SWEET AND SAVORY
GRILLED CHEESE SANDWICH

SPICY CHEESE STRATA

HAM AND SPINACH QUICHE

BROWN SUGAR BAKED COUNTRY HAM

HERB ROASTED TURKEY BREAST

SWEET POTATO PANCAKES

HOMEMADE SAUSAGE

SAUTÉED POTATOES AND ONIONS

CHOCOLATE WAFFLES WITH BERRIES
AND YOGURT

BUTTERMILK-PECAN BREAD

You sure don't miss the egg yolks in this cheesy, creamy omelet—one of my favorite lunch, brunch and late-night meals. You can change the cheeses to any you have on hand and if you don't have shallots, use onion or scallion. I also like to add whatever vegetables I have available to add a little color. My most favorite garnish is a heaping tablespoon of LaBelle Sweet Hot Jalapeño Relish on every wedge.

SERVES 6 TO 8

18 large egg whites

½ cup milk

Salt and black pepper or to taste

2 tablespoons butter, at room temperature

1 small shallot, peeled and minced

3 trimmed, cooked asparagus stalks, cut into 1-inch pieces on the bias, optional

1 cup diced fresh tomato, optional

1 cup grated sharp Cheddar cheese

½ cup grated Parmesan cheese

1 tablespoon minced parsley

EGG WHITE AND CHEESE OMELET

1. Preheat the oven to 350°F.

2. Combine the egg whites and milk with salt and pepper in a mixing bowl, whisking until frothy. Set aside.

(continued)

3. Heat the butter in an ovenproof 10-inch nonstick frying pan over medium heat. Add the shallot and sauté for about 2 minutes or until soft and fragrant. If using, stir in the asparagus and tomato, season with salt and pepper, and sauté for another minute. Pour the egg mixture into the pan and briefly stir with a spatula to blend. Reduce the heat to medium-low and cook for about 2 minutes or until the eggs begin to set. Sprinkle the cheeses over the top, season with a little more pepper, and carefully push a spatula under the edge of the omelet to keep it from sticking to the pan.

4. Transfer the omelet to the preheated oven and bake for about 7 minutes or until it puffs and is cooked through

5. Remove from the oven and carefully slide the omelet onto a serving plate and sprinkle with parsley. Let stand about 2 minutes before cutting into wedges.

What better way to start off the day than with a hearty breakfast sandwich of eggs with cheese and sausage on a biscuit? Those fast-food joints ain't got nothing on this! It's so good and so filling you may just have to skip lunch. It's a bit healthier and tastier than most—or at least I think so. This recipe makes 8 little sandwiches, but I'm telling you, everyone will want seconds, so be prepared to go back to the stove.

If you want to put in a little extra effort, cook up some of my cheese biscuits (see page 46)—these sandwiches taste great with them.

MAKES 8

One 9-ounce can
    of your favorite
    biscuits

8 turkey sausage
    patties, preferably
    my homemade (see
    Page 167)

1 tablespoon minced
    onion

1 teaspoon minced
    garlic

4 large eggs, beaten

2 tablespoons milk

Salt and freshly ground
    black pepper to taste

½ cup grated sharp
    cheddar cheese

HEARTY BREAKFAST SANDWICHES

1. Preheat the oven to 200°F.

2. Bake the biscuits according to the package directions. Keep warm in the preheated oven.

(continued)

3. If necessary, trim the turkey patties to the exact size of the biscuits. Place the turkey sausage patties in a medium nonstick frying pan over low heat. Fry, turning occasionally, for about 5 minutes or until nicely browned and cooked through.

4. Transfer to a double layer of paper towel to drain. When drained, place on a small pan in the preheated oven to keep warm.

5. Spray a medium nonstick frying pan with nonstick vegetable spray. Place over medium heat and add the onion and garlic. Cook, stirring frequently, for about 3 minutes or just until translucent.

6. Whisk the eggs and milk together and then pour the eggs into the frying pan and reduce the heat to low. Cook, stirring occasionally from the outside edge to the center, for about 4 minutes or until the eggs are almost set, but still quite moist.

7. Season with salt and pepper and place the cheese on top of the cooked eggs.

8. Split the biscuits in half, crosswise. Place a turkey sausage patty on the bottom half of each biscuit. Place an equal portion of the egg/cheese mixture on top of the sausage on each biscuit bottom. Place the biscuit top on each one and serve.

*T*his is a Dagwood-type of grilled cheese sandwich. You can make it with any type of cheese, you can add mustard and pickles, or replace the honey with honey mustard. If you have a really sweet tooth, you can substitute your favorite jam for the honey.

MAKES 1

2 slices whole wheat bread

1 slice Monterey Jack cheese

1 tablespoon honey

1 slice sharp Cheddar cheese

3 strips cooked bacon

2 thin slices ripe, juicy tomato

1 tablespoon butter, at room temperature

SWEET AND SAVORY GRILLED CHEESE SANDWICH

1. Place a slice of the bread on a clean, flat work surface.

2. Top with a slice of Jack cheese. Drizzle honey over the cheese and top with a slice of Cheddar cheese. Top with 3 strips of bacon and a couple of slices of tomato. Top with a slice of bread.

3. Spread butter on both sides of the sandwich.

4. Place a small nonstick frying pan over medium heat. Add the sandwich and cook for about 3 minutes or until the bread is golden brown and the cheese has begun to melt.

5. Carefully turn and cook for another 2 minutes or so or until the remaining side is golden and the cheese is getting oozy.

6. Remove from the pan, cut in half, on the diagonal, and serve with some sweet pickles on the side.

As you might have guessed, I'm a pretty busy gal. But, I always have time to cook for family and friends. One of the reasons that I can do so easily is that I always have something on hand to feed a crowd. This dish is one you can make when you have some free time, and then freeze it for safekeeping until you're called upon to make a last-minute, time-crunch meal.

SERVES 6

12 ounces sharp Cheddar cheese, grated

12 ounces Monterey Jack cheese, grated

12 slices stale white or whole wheat bread

3 tablespoons butter

8 large eggs

2 cups heavy cream

1½ cups milk

3 tablespoons grated onion

1 teaspoon dry mustard powder

1 teaspoon LaBelle Rich Red Hot Sauce

1 teaspoon Worcestershire sauce

¼ teaspoon paprika

LaBelle Seasoned Sea Salt and Seasoned Pepper to taste

SPICY CHEESE STRATA

1. Generously grease a 3 quart casserole.

2. If baking immediately, preheat the oven to 350°F.

3. Combine the 2 cheeses.

4. Remove and discard the bread crusts. Cut the bread into small cubes.

5. Heat the butter in a large frying pan over medium heat. Add the bread and sauté for about 3 minutes or until the bread has absorbed the butter. Remove from the heat.

6. Place half of the bread cubes in the bottom of the prepared casserole. Place half of the combined cheeses on top of the bread cubes and, using half of the remaining bread cubes, follow with a layer of bread cubes. Top with the remaining cheeses and a final layer of bread cubes.

7. Combine the eggs with the cream and milk, onion, mustard, hot sauce, Worcestershire sauce, paprika, and seasoning salt and pepper to taste, whisking to blend. Pour the mixture over the bread and cheese in the casserole.

8. Place in the preheated oven and bake for about 45 minutes or until golden brown and puffed. Remove from the oven and serve piping hot.

3 large eggs

1½ cups heavy cream, half-and-half, or whole milk

1 cup finely diced cooked ham

1 cup thawed, frozen chopped spinach, squeezed almost dry

½ cup grated Gruyère or other cheese of choice

½ teaspoon LaBelle Hot Flash Hot Sauce

Salt to taste

One 9-inch prepared pie shell

Some people say "real men don't eat quiche." Well, I've never met a real man who passed up my quiche! The great thing about a quiche is that if you have some ready-made piecrusts on hand, you can almost always quickly put one together if your pantry is stocked like mine is. All you need is a salad to go with it, and you have a complete meal. As a healthy variation, you can also make a quiche using egg replacement and 2% milk, but you will have to add a tablespoon of flour to help the mixture set.

SERVES 4 TO 6

HAM AND SPINACH QUICHE

1. Preheat the oven to 375°F.

2. Combine the eggs and cream in a mixing bowl, whisking to blend well. Stir in the ham, spinach, and cheese. Season with hot sauce and salt to taste. Carefully pour into the pie shell and transfer to the preheated oven. Bake for about 30 minutes or until the pastry is golden brown and the center is set.

3. Remove from the oven and let rest for 10 minutes before cutting into wedges and serving.

A gathering is really special when there's a big, beautiful ham at the center of the table. And, if it's an old-fashioned country ham, that's even better. If you've never had one, a country ham is one that has been dry-cured in a salt-based mix of sodium nitrate, sugars, spices and herbs, usually in Virginia, Kentucky, Georgia or Tennessee. Once dry-cured, the hams are smoked and then aged for up to a year. The meat is very salty and firm, so the ham must be soaked thoroughly before cooking. My cooking method results in a slightly salty ham, with a beautiful, sweet glaze that will stand out on any table.

ONE 14-POUND HAM

One 12- to 14-pound
country ham

2 teaspoons whole
cloves

3 cups apple cider or
apple juice

3 cups pineapple juice

One 1-pound box
dark brown sugar

One 16-ounce bottle
dark corn syrup

BROWN SUGAR BAKED COUNTRY HAM

1. Place the ham in a deep pot (or, better yet, in a very clean sink) and cover with cold water. Soak, changing the soaking water once, for 12 hours.

2. Preheat the oven to 325°F.

3. Drain well, pat dry, and trim off the dry skin and excess fat.

(continued)

4. Randomly insert the cloves into the ham. Then, place the ham, fat side up, in a large roasting pan. Pour the cider and pineapple juice over the ham, cover, and place in the preheated oven. Bake for 90 minutes.

5. Remove the ham from the oven, uncover, and carefully coat the entire top of the ham with a layer of the brown sugar. Then, pour the syrup over the brown sugar, taking care not to disturb the coating.

6. Return the ham to the oven and continue to bake, basting with the pan juices every 15 minutes, for about another 2 hours or until an instant-read thermometer inserted into the thickest part reads 160°F.

7. Remove from the oven and let rest, basting with the pan juices every 5 minutes, for 15 minutes before slicing.

*I*f you have a family that only eats white meat when the big bird is the feature, this is the perfect solution. Splitting the breast allows very quick cooking, keeping it on the bone ensures that the meat stays moist, and the herbs add great flavor. This is also a great way to always have the makings of a turkey BLT on hand. Place the turkey breast on the table, surrounded by crisp turkey bacon, juicy sliced tomatoes, lettuce and condiments, and let everyone make their own sandwich.

For a special gravy, once the turkey is roasted, transfer the pan juices to a small saucepan. Dissolve 1 tablespoon of cornstarch in 2 tablespoons of cold water, add it to the pan juices, and place over low heat. Cook, stirring, for about 4 minutes or until thick, and you'll have an instant gravy.

SERVES 6

One 6-pound bone-in turkey breast, rinsed, split, and skin removed

2 tablespoons olive oil

2 tablespoons melted butter

4 garlic cloves, peeled and crushed

2 teaspoons chopped fresh sage or 1 teaspoon dried sage

2 teaspoons chopped fresh thyme or 1 teaspoon dried thyme

2 teaspoons chopped fresh rosemary or 1 teaspoon dried rosemary

Salt and freshly ground pepper to taste

1 teaspoon paprika

1 cup low-sodium chicken broth

HERB-ROASTED TURKEY BREAST

(continued)

1. Preheat the oven to 375°F.

2. Pat the turkey breast halves dry and place them in a roasting pan.

3. Combine the oil and butter with the garlic, sage, thyme, rosemary, and salt and pepper to taste. When well combined, rub the mixture onto the flesh underneath the skin by carefully lifting up the skin and inserting your fingers under it.

4. Season the skin with salt and pepper to taste and lightly coat with paprika.

5. Place the breasts in a roasting pan along with the broth. Transfer to the preheated oven and roast, basting occasionally, for about 1 hour or until the juices run clear when the meat is pierced with the point of a small, sharp knife and an instant-read thermometer reads 160°F when inserted into the thickest part.

6. Remove from the oven and allow to rest for about 10 minutes before carving.

I love my sweets, but I try not to eat the candied ones that I grew up on. This is one of my ways of enjoying the sweet flavored meal, without the addition of unnecessary sugar. If you leave out the onion, you can serve the pancakes with applesauce, apple butter or syrup.

SERVES 6

6 medium sweet potatoes, peeled and grated

1 cup grated onion

2 large eggs

2 tablespoons all-purpose flour

¼ teaspoon baking powder

Salt and white pepper to taste

Approximately ½ cup vegetable oil

Non-fat sour cream for serving

SWEET POTATO PANCAKES

1. Preheat the oven to its lowest setting.

2. Line a rimmed baking pan with a double layer of paper towel. Set aside.

3. Combine the potatoes, onion, and eggs in a mixing bowl. Stir in the flour, baking powder, and salt and pepper to taste.

4. Heat part of the oil in a large, heavy frying pan—cast iron is the best—over medium-high heat. When very hot, but not smoking, add the potato mixture by the heaping spoonfuls—you want to make pancakes about 3 inches in diameter. Do not crowd the pan. Lower the heat to medium and fry the pancakes for about 3 minutes or until the bottom is brown. Turn and fry for another 3 minutes or until golden.

(continued)

165

5. Transfer the cooked pancakes to the prepared baking pan and place in the warm oven to keep warm while you continue frying pancakes. Wipe the pan clean, if too many browned bits are in the oil start with fresh oil, if necessary.

6. Serve hot, with sour cream, if desired.

*O*nce you've made this sausage, you'll never pick up another pre-made link or patty. It's so easy to do—you can double or triple this recipe and keep the patties on hand in the freezer for early morning breakfast, weekend brunch, or a late-night sandwich.

If you prefer an all-pork sausage, replace the turkey with a pork shoulder cut.

MAKES ABOUT 2 ½ POUNDS

2 pounds boneless, skinless turkey breast or a mixture of breast and thigh meat

8 ounces pork fatback, trimmed of rind

1 tablespoon ground black pepper

1½ tablespoons poultry seasoning

1 tablespoon LaBelle Diced Fine Jalapeños

2 teaspoons salt

Pinch ground cloves

½ cup cold water

HOMEMADE SAUSAGE

1. Cut the meat and fatback into small pieces. Place in the bowl of a food processor fitted with the metal blade and, using quick on and off turns, coarsely chop.

2. Scrape the chopped mixture into a mixing bowl and add the pepper, poultry seasoning, jalapeños, salt, and cloves along with ¼ cup cold water. Using your hands, squeeze the mixture together to completely blend.

3. Form the mixture into serving-size patties and either fry as you would any sausage or pack the patties into a container, in single layers separated by freezer paper, and freeze for up to 3 months.

¼ cup vegetable oil, olive oil, melted butter or, the best of all, bacon fat if your diet allows

1 large onion—sweet, yellow or red, peeled and diced

6 large all-purpose potatoes, peeled and cubed or sliced

A good dose of La Belle Organic Blended Seasoned Sea Salt and coarse ground black pepper

*T*his is a perfect combo for brunch, lunch, late night—you name it, and it works like a charm. I guess everybody's mom has a recipe for this dish—some use raw potatoes, some use cooked, some cubed, some sliced—but I don't think it matters what you start with, as long as the result is slightly crisp potatoes and onions with really good caramelization.

SERVES 6

SAUTÉED POTATOES AND ONIONS

Heat the oil in a large, heavy frying pan—cast iron is the best—over medium-high heat. When very hot, add the onion and sauté for 3 minutes. Add the potatoes along with the salt and pepper, stirring to combine. Cover, lower the heat, and cook for about 20 minutes or until the bottom is crusty and brown. Uncover, and break up the potatoes, turning them so that the top pieces are on the bottom. Continue to cook, stirring occasionally, for another 15 minutes or until the potatoes are crisp and the onions are golden.

When I was younger, I would often find myself with friends and family sitting around the kitchen table talking late at night (well, technically, really early in the morning), and we almost always wound up getting hungry and eating the same thing—chicken and waffles. Yes, not the most common combo of foods, but if you've had it before, then you know how incredible it is. Well, I've abandoned that combo for a new, healthier one that I think is just as good—my chocolate waffles and berries.

You can also cut the waffles into quarters, place a scoop of ice cream on top, drizzle with chocolate sauce, add a sprig of mint and you have dessert on the spot!

SERVES 6

2 cups all-purpose flour

¼ cup sugar

2 tablespoons cocoa powder

1 tablespoon baking powder

½ teaspoon ground cinnamon

Pinch salt

2 large eggs, separated

2 cups 2% milk

¼ cup melted unsalted butter or vegetable oil

3 cups sliced strawberries or whole raspberries, blueberries, or blackberries

2 cups nonfat vanilla yogurt

CHOCOLATE WAFFLES WITH BERRIES AND YOGURT

(continued)

1. Combine the flour, sugar, cocoa powder, baking powder, cinnamon, and salt in a mixing bowl.

2. Place the egg whites in a small mixing bowl and, using a handheld mixer, beat until stiff peaks form.

3. Add the egg yolks, milk and butter (or oil) to the flour mixture, beating to blend. When a batter has formed, fold in the egg whites.

4. Bake in a preheated waffle iron according to the manufacturer's directions. This recipe should yield six waffles.

5. Serve topped with berries and yogurt.

*T*his is so easy to put together in the morning and the sweet-nutty smell coming from the oven will bring even late-sleepers to the table. This bread also freezes well, so don't hesitate to make a couple of loaves to have on hand. A quick pop in the microwave and the same wonderful aroma will fill the house.

MAKES ONE 9-INCH LOAF

2 ¼ cups sifted all-purpose flour

1 cup light brown sugar

2 teaspoons baking powder

½ teaspoon baking soda

½ teaspoon ground cinnamon

¼ teaspoon ground nutmeg

¼ teaspoon salt

1 large egg, beaten

1 cup buttermilk

2 tablespoons canola oil or melted butter

1 cup chopped pecans or other favorite nuts

BUTTERMILK-PECAN BREAD

1. Preheat the oven to 350°F.

2. Lightly coat a 9-inch loaf pan with nonstick vegetable spray and flour. Set aside.

(continued)

3. Sift the flour, sugar, baking powder, baking soda, cinnamon, nutmeg and salt into a medium mixing bowl. In another bowl, beat the egg, buttermilk and oil together, and then stir the liquid into the flour mixture to just combine. Stir in the nuts.

4. Scrape the mixture into the prepared pan and place in the preheated oven. Bake for about 40 minutes or until a cake tester inserted into the center comes out clean. Remove from the oven and place on a wire rack to cool for 10 minutes before removing from the pan. Serve warm or at room temperature.

Happy Holidays

Sweet Butternut Squash Soup

Miss Patti's Leg of Lamb

Tender-to-the-Bone Rib Roast

Stuffed Cornish Game Hens

Black-Eyed Peas and Rice

Miss Patti's Favorite Lima Beans

Corn Pudding

Creamy Sautéed Spinach

Creamy Garlic Mashed Potatoes

Cranberry-Pineapple Relish

Twice-Baked Sweet Potatoes

5 cups chicken broth

1 cup chopped shallots

1 teaspoon grated fresh ginger
or ¼ teaspoon ground

Three 12-ounces packages
frozen puréed squash,
thawed

Approximately ¾ cup honey

¼ teaspoon ground nutmeg

¼ teaspoon ground cinnamon

¼ teaspoon curry powder

Salt and ground white pepper
to taste

6 tablespoons nonfat
unflavored or vanilla
yogurt, optional

2 tablespoons minced chives,
optional

This is a wonderful celebratory soup and serves as a light introduction to a heavy meal. Even better, it can be made in advance and heated just before serving—a terrific help to a busy holiday cook. It is difficult to give an exact amount of honey for the recipe, since some squash is sweeter than others. You'll just have to use your judgment when adding it. If you can't eat honey, sweeten the soup with your favorite sugar substitute. You'll note that I haven't added any heat, but, if you'd like, a drop or two of LaBelle Pepper Clear Mild Pepper Sauce would add just the right amount of zing.

SERVES 6

SWEET BUTTERNUT SQUASH SOUP

1. Heat the broth in a large saucepan over medium heat. Add the shallots and ginger and bring to a simmer. Lower the heat and simmer for about 5 minutes or until the shallots have softened. Stir in the squash, honey, nutmeg, cinnamon, and curry. Raise the heat and again bring to a simmer. Season with salt and white pepper to taste and simmer for 15 minutes.

2. Remove from heat and working in batches, pour the soup into a blender. Process, holding down the lid with a kitchen towel to keep the steam from lifting it off of the blender jar, until smooth. The soup may be made up to this point and stored, covered and refrigerated, for up to 3 days or frozen for up to 3 months. If frozen, thaw before using.

3. When ready to serve, place the soup in a clean saucepan. Taste and, if necessary, add additional honey, salt, and white pepper. Bring to a simmer.

4. Remove from the heat and serve, garnished with a dollop of yogurt in the center and chives sprinkled over the top, if desired.

*T*his is a beautiful way to celebrate the spring holidays. Everyone loves my leg of lamb—juicy and tender, with a rich gravy on the side. I like to add the mint for just a hint of the traditional Greek flavor often associated with lamb. If you like, you can add some extra chopped mint and a teaspoon of lemon juice to the gravy for a very authentic Greek taste.

SERVES 6

½ bunch flat leaf parsley, well-washed and dried

One 3½ pound oven-ready leg of lamb, silverskin and excess fat removed

4 cloves garlic, peeled and slivered

2 tablespoons "lite" olive oil

5 tablespoons unsalted butter, at room temperature

LaBelle Seasoned Sea Salt to taste

1 teaspoon cracked black pepper

2 ribs celery, well-washed and chopped

1 large carrot, peeled, trimmed, and chopped

1 medium onion, peeled and chopped

1 bay leaf

1 cup chicken broth

2 tablespoons chopped fresh mint

1 cup dry red wine

Salt and pepper to taste

MISS PATTI'S LEG OF LAMB

1. Preheat the oven to 425°F.

2. Separate the parsley leaves from the stems. Chop the leaves. Measure out 2 tablespoons and 1 tablespoon and separately reserve them. Separately reserve the stems.

176

3. Using a small sharp knife, randomly make little cuts into the meat. Insert a sliver of garlic into each one. Rub the exterior with the oil, followed by 3 tablespoons of the butter. Liberally season the lamb with salt and cracked pepper.

4. Place a roasting pan on the stovetop over high heat. Add the lamb and sear, turning frequently, for about 8 minutes or until well-browned on all sides. Remove the pan from the heat and push the celery, carrot, onion, bay leaf and parsley stems under the lamb. Add the broth and transfer to the oven.

5. Roast the lamb, turning once, for 20 minutes. Add the reserved 2 tablespoons chopped parsley along with the mint and continue roasting for another 20 minutes. Turn the lamb and continue roasting for another 15 minutes or until an instant-read thermometer reads 155°F for medium. The lamb will continue to cook as it rests. For well-done, you will need to roast for another 10 to 15 minutes or until the thermometer reads 165°F.

6. Remove from the oven and transfer to a serving platter. Tent lightly with aluminum foil and let rest for 15 minutes before carving.

7. Ladle off the excess fat in the roasting pan. Place the pan on the stovetop over medium-high heat. Add the wine, scraping the bottom of the pan with a wooden spoon to lift up any browned bits. Bring to a boil, then immediately lower the heat and simmer for about 5 minutes or until the liquid has reduced and thickened slightly. Remove the bay leaf and parsley stems and carefully pour the liquid into a blender jar. Holding the lid down with a kitchen towel to keep the heat from pushing it off, process until smooth.

8. Strain the purée into a clean saucepan over medium heat and bring to a simmer. Whisk in the remaining 2 tablespoons butter. When the butter has been incorporated into the gravy, taste, and, if necessary, season with salt and pepper. Remove from the heat and stir in the remaining 1 tablespoon parsley.

9. Carve the lamb and serve the gravy on the side.

One 5-pound (3 rib)
standing rib roast

2 teaspoons LaBelle
Seasoned Sea Salt

1 teaspoon LaBelle
Seasoned Pepper

1 teaspoon dried parsley
flakes

1 teaspoon garlic powder

1 teaspoon onion powder

I guess that this is a bit over-the-top, but what an amazing presentation this roast makes! The beautiful crust that forms as it roasts makes it even more impressive. And, of course, meat eaters always love to gnaw on the meaty rib bones. You can also cut the meat from the bones and then make another meal out of the bones—just coat them with a mustard crust and bake for about 20 minutes. You'll have a great, finger-lickin' meal made from leftovers.

SERVES 6

TENDER-TO-THE-BONE RIB ROAST

1. Allow the roast to come to room temperature.

2. Preheat the oven to 375°F.

3. Combine the salt, pepper, parsley, garlic powder, and onion powder in a small bowl.

4. Place the roast on a rack, fatty side up, in a large roasting pan. Rub the salt mixture into the fatty side of the roast. If the pan has a lid, cover it or tightly enclose the entire pan with aluminum foil.

5. Place in the preheated oven and roast for 90 minutes. Turn the oven off and leave the roast in the turned off oven for 15 minutes.

6. Remove from the oven, uncover, and serve.

*S*erving individual birds really says "this is a special dinner." These are particularly inviting with their sweet, fruity stuffing, which is further accented with the flavor of the apricot basting sauce. If you don't have both pecans and walnuts on hand, just use whatever you have—you just need the crunchiness that the nuts add.

SERVES 6

½ cup apricot nectar

1 tablespoon "lite" soy sauce

1 teaspoon garlic powder

1 teaspoon paprika

Salt and freshly ground black pepper to taste

Six 1½ pound Cornish game hens

Fruit and Nut Stuffing (recipe follows)

STUFFED CORNISH GAME HENS

1. Combine the apricot nectar, soy sauce, garlic powder, and paprika with salt and pepper to taste in a small bowl, whisking to blend well. Set aside.

2. Rinse the hens under cold, running water and pat dry.

3. Place about ½ cup of the stuffing in the cavity of each bird. Using kitchen twine, tie the legs together to make a neat closure.

4. Place the hens, breast side up, on the rack of a large roasting pan. Using a pastry brush, generously coat each bird with the reserved apricot nectar mixture. Pour the remaining apricot nectar mixture into the roasting pan along with 1 cup of water.

(continued)

5. Cover the pan with aluminum foil and place in the preheated oven. Roast for 20 minutes. Uncover and continue to roast, basting with the pan juices from time to time, for about 20 minutes or until golden brown and an instant-read thermometer inserted into the thickest part reads 165°F.

6. Remove from the oven and let rest for about 5 minutes before serving.

FRUIT AND NUT STUFFING

2 cups herb-flavored stuffing croutons

½ cup chopped canned apricots

½ cup chopped dried figs

½ cup golden raisins

½ cup halved seedless green grapes

¼ cup chopped pecans or walnuts

1 tablespoon chopped fresh flat leaf parsley

½ teaspoon garlic powder

½ teaspoon LaBelle Seasoned Sea Salt

⅛ cup melted butter

3 tablespoons apricot nectar

1. Combine the croutons, apricots, figs, raisins, grapes, pecans, parsley, garlic powder and seasoning salt in a mixing bowl. Pour the melted butter and apricot nectar over the top and toss to combine. You want a mixture that is moist, but not wet.

2. Use as directed in the recipe.

*B*lack-eyed peas and rice is also known as "Hoppin' John" and, if eaten on New Year's Day, it is said to bring you luck the whole year ahead. It can be a side dish or a main course. If using it as a main course, this recipe might feed 3 people—that is, if they aren't too hungry. This is a Southern favorite that many people outside of the South don't quite get. I think it is the earthy taste of the peas that you are either born to love or hate. Whatever the case, I do believe that a big bowl of it will bring you luck!

SERVES 6

1 pound dried black-eyed peas

1 tablespoon vegetable oil

1 cup diced cooked lean ham

1 medium onion, peeled and chopped

1 cup chopped green bell pepper

1 teaspoon minced garlic

2 bay leaves

1 tablespoon chopped fresh flat leaf parsley

1 tablespoon LaBelle Hot Flash Hot Sauce

Salt and black pepper to taste

3 cups cooked rice

BLACK-EYED PEAS AND RICE

1. Rinse the peas under cold, running water.

2. Place in a large saucepan with 5 cups of boiling water. Place over high heat and bring to a boil. Boil for 3 minutes; then, remove from the heat, cover, and set aside for 4 hours to soak.

(continued)

3. Drain the peas in a colander and rinse under cold, running water. Set aside.

4. Heat the oil in a large, deep frying pan. Add the ham and place over medium-high heat. Cook, stirring frequently, for about 4 minutes or until the ham has begun to brown.

5. Add the onion, bell pepper, and garlic and sauté for about 4 minutes or until the vegetables have softened. Stir in the reserved black-eyed peas along with the bay leaves, parsley, Hot Flash, and salt and pepper to taste along with 4 cups of water.

6. Cover and bring to a simmer. Lower the heat and simmer for about 35 minutes or until the peas are very tender.

7. Remove and discard the bay leaves.

8. Add the rice and cook, stirring occasionally, for an additional 5 minutes or until all of the liquid has been absorbed.

9. Remove from the heat and serve.

1 pound dried lima or butter beans

2 tablespoons "lite" olive oil

1 medium onion, peeled and finely chopped

1 cup diced celery

1 cup diced carrots

1 cup diced leeks

1 teaspoon minced garlic

1½ pounds smoked turkey wings, cut into large pieces

1½ tablespoons light brown sugar

6 cups low-sodium chicken broth or water

Salt and pepper to taste

2 tablespoons chopped fresh parsley

LaBelle Rich Red Hot Sauce to taste, optional

The smoked turkey adds great flavor, as well as some hearty goodness, to the delicate beans. You can also use fresh or frozen lima beans with absolutely fabulous results. The dish won't be as hearty, but it will be just as flavorful.

SERVES 6

MISS PATTI'S FAVORITE LIMA BEANS

1. Place the beans in cold water to cover and set aside to soak for at least 8 hours or overnight.

(continued)

2. Drain the beans and place in a medium saucepan with water to cover by 2 inches. Place over medium-high heat and bring to a boil. Lower the heat and simmer for 30 minutes. Remove from the heat and set aside.

3. While the beans are simmering, heat the oil in a Dutch oven over medium heat. Add the onion, celery, carrots, leeks, and garlic and cook, stirring frequently, for about 4 minutes or just until the vegetables are beginning to soften. Add the turkey wings and sugar along with the broth (or water). Place over medium-high heat and bring to a boil. Lower the heat and cook at a gentle simmer for 30 minutes.

4. Drain the beans and add them to the turkey mixture. Raise the heat and return the mixture to a boil. Lower the heat, cover, leaving the lid ajar, and cook at a gentle simmer for about 1 hour or until the beans are tender.

5. Uncover, season with salt and pepper to taste, and cook for an additional 5 minutes.

6. Remove from the heat, stir in the parsley and, if using, the hot sauce, and serve.

*T*his is an old-fashioned side dish that I love to serve for the holidays. It is even great in the summer, made with kernels from left over grilled corn on the cob. If you have cholesterol concerns, substitute egg replacement for the yolks and olive oil for the butter.

SERVES 6 TO 8

3 cups thawed frozen corn kernels

2 large eggs, separated

¼ cup finely diced red bell pepper

¼ cup finely diced green bell pepper

2 tablespoons melted butter

2 tablespoons all-purpose flour

½ teaspoon LaBelle Rich Red Hot Sauce

1 cup hot 2% milk

Salt and pepper to taste

CORN PUDDING

1. Preheat the oven to 350°F.

2. Generously grease a 1½ quart casserole.

3. Combine the corn with the egg yolks, bell peppers, butter, flour, and hot sauce in a mixing bowl. When blended, stir in the milk and season with salt and pepper to taste.

4. Place the egg whites in a small mixing bowl and, using a handheld electric mixer, beat until soft peaks form. Fold the beaten egg whites into the corn mixture and pour into the prepared casserole.

5. Place in the preheated oven and bake for about 45 minutes or until just set and golden brown on top. Remove from the oven and serve.

2 tablespoons butter

2 tablespoons olive oil

1 cup minced onions

1 teaspoon minced garlic

Three 16-ounce packages frozen
chopped spinach, well-drained

¼ cup sour cream

¼ cup heavy cream

3 tablespoons grated Parmesan
cheese

2 tablespoons minced fresh flat
leaf parsley

1 teaspoon seasoned salt

Freshly ground black pepper to taste

Pinch ground nutmeg

*M*y creamed spinach can go toe-to-toe with any served in a fancy steakhouse. It is so creamy and rich that even spinach-haters will love it. I always serve it at holiday time because it's a side dish that can go with just about anything.

If you like, you can replace the frozen spinach with 3 pounds of well-washed, chopped fresh spinach, or with baby spinach leaves.

SERVES 6

CREAMY SAUTÉED SPINACH

1. Heat the butter and olive oil in a large frying pan over low heat. Add the onions and garlic and cook, stirring frequently, for about 10 minutes or just until the onions are translucent.

2. Add the spinach and cook for 3 minutes, stirring frequently.

3. Stir in the sour cream and heavy cream, stirring to blend. Add the Parmesan cheese and parsley and cook, stirring frequently, for about 4 minutes or just until hot. Do not boil or the fat will begin to separate.

4. Stir in seasoned salt and pepper to taste along with the nutmeg, remove from the heat, and serve.

These are very, very garlicky. If you're not a fan of the raw garlic taste, cut the cloves into pieces and cook them along with the potatoes. Or, roast the whole head, wrapped in aluminum foil, for about 20 minutes in a 350°F oven—then squeeze the sweet garlic pulp into the potatoes, beating it in so it blends well. Each of these will result in a different taste, all of them delicious.

SERVES 6

6 large Idaho potatoes, peeled and diced

1 cup heavy cream

½ cup butter

½ cup roasted garlic purée (see Note)

3 tablespoons sour cream

Salt and freshly ground black pepper to taste

CREAMY GARLIC MASHED POTATOES

1. Place the potatoes in cold, salted water to cover over high heat. Cover and bring to a boil. Lower the heat and simmer for about 20 minutes or until the potatoes are tender when pierced with the point of a small, sharp knife.

2. While the potatoes are cooking, heat the cream and butter in a small pan over low heat. Do not boil.

3. Remove the potatoes from the heat and drain well. Place in a mixing bowl. Add the garlic and sour cream, beating to blend. Slowly begin to add the reserved hot cream, beating until the potatoes are fluffy and smooth. You may not need all of the cream.

4. Transfer to a serving bowl and serve hot. *(continued)*

NOTE: You can buy roasted garlic purée, but it's easy to make and tastes a lot better when you do it yourself. Cut a bit of the top off of the whole head to reveal the flesh in the cloves. This will make it very easy to push the roasted flesh out of the skin. Generously coat with olive oil, wrap in foil, and roast for about 20 minutes or until very soft. Unwrap and, using your fingertips, push the flesh out of the skin from the root end up. One large head should yield about 3 tablespoons of roasted purée.

*E*veryone has their favorite cranberry sauce and this is mine. I've taken out all of the sugar usually required by using apple juice concentrate and unsweetened (but still sweet) canned pineapple and a sugar replacement. It freezes nicely so it can be served with the Easter ham or lamb, as well as with the Christmas turkey.

MAKES ABOUT 1 QUART

One 1-pound package fresh cranberries

One 10-ounce can unsweetened crushed pineapple

1¼ cups apple juice concentrate

1 tablespoon LaBelle Pepper Clear Mild Pepper Sauce

1 tablespoon freshly grated orange zest

½ teaspoon ground ginger

2 tablespoons sugar replacement or to taste

CRANBERRY-PINEAPPLE RELISH

1. Combine the cranberries, pineapples, concentrate, hot sauce, orange zest, and ginger in a medium heavy bottomed saucepan over medium heat. Stir in the sugar replacement and bring to a simmer. Lower the heat and cook at a bare simmer for about 30 minutes or until the cranberries have popped and the mixture is slightly thick.

2. Remove from the heat and allow to cool. Store, tightly covered and refrigerated, for up to 1 week or freeze for up to 6 months.

3 large sweet potatoes, well-washed and dried

2 tablespoons vegetable oil

2 teaspoons ground cinnamon

½ teaspoon ground nutmeg

½ teaspoon salt plus more to taste

½ cup fat-free sour cream

2 tablespoons unsalted butter, at room temperature

2 tablespoons pure maple syrup

1 tablespoon light brown sugar

Ground white pepper and salt to taste

¼ cup chopped pecans or walnuts

*I*f you use very large sweet potatoes, they can be used as a main course for lunch. Just serve them with a salad and frosty glasses of my Sweet Tea with Lemon and Lime (see page 151), sweetened with sugar substitute for people watching their sugar intake.

SERVES 6

TWICE-BAKED SWEET POTATOES

1. Preheat the oven to 375°F.

2. Line a cookie sheet with aluminum foil. Cut the potatoes in half, lengthwise, and place them, cut side down, on the foil-lined pan.

3. Using vegetable oil, lightly coat the skin side of the potatoes. Then sprinkle with cinnamon, nutmeg, and a little salt. Using a kitchen fork, randomly pierce the skin to allow the steam to escape as they bake.

4. Place in the preheated oven and bake for about 40 minutes or until the potatoes are tender when pierced with the point of a small, sharp knife.

5. Remove from the oven and place on a wire rack to cool. (Do not turn the oven off unless you are going to finish the potatoes at a later time.)

6. When the potatoes are cool enough to handle, carefully scoop out the flesh, keeping the shells intact. Set the potato shells aside.

7. Raise the oven temperature to 400°F.

8. Place the potato flesh in a mixing bowl and beat with a wooden spoon until quite smooth. Add the sour cream along with butter, maple syrup, and sugar beating until very smooth. (You can use a handheld electric mixer to do this, also.) Season with salt and white pepper to taste.

9. Spoon an equal portion of the potato mixture into each half shell, mounding it a bit in the center. Sprinkle each one with some nuts and place on a non-stick rimmed baking sheet in the preheated oven. Bake for about 10 minutes or until the tops are lightly browned and the potatoes are heated through.

10. Remove from the oven and sprinkle the tops with pecans, walnuts, or coconut, if desired. Serve hot.

Cakes, Pies and Other Things I Shouldn't Eat

*L*ike many people out there, I have a sweet tooth—or, really, a whole bunch of sweet teeth! I don't believe a meal is complete without dessert. Of course, I cannot always indulge the way I want to. But, again, the good life is about enjoying life to the fullest, and that means not depriving myself of a single thing. So, instead of the whole piece of pie, or the whole slice of cake, I will have a few forkfuls and I'm done.

What I have also learned to do is to substitute the bad things for the good. There are many healthy alternatives to sugar and heaps of butter, and I have learned to use them in my recipes. So I get all of the fun and flavor without worrying about my health.

I've stayed true to most of the original recipes in this chapter, which are really for those who don't have any serious health issues or who, like me, need to cheat every now and then. But I also have a recipe or two, like the You Really Can Eat It Carrot Cake, which you *can* really eat without the guilt. Either way, you're in for a real treat!

PERFECT CHOCOLATE CAKE

COCONUT CAKE

APRICOT-BRANDY POUND CAKE

BLACKBERRY JAM-SPICE CAKE

YOU REALLY CAN EAT IT CARROT CAKE

CREAM CAKE WITH BERRIES AND BANANAS

FRIED APPLE PIE

BEAN PIE

PEAR DUMPLINGS

DIANE'S SPECIAL OCCASION
BREAD PUDDING

MERINGUE RING WITH BERRIES

GOOD FOR YOU FRUIT SALAD

3 large egg yolks, at room temperature

½ cup milk

1 cup packed light brown sugar

4 ounces unsweetened chocolate,
    chopped into small pieces

¼ teaspoon Jamaican allspice

½ cup heavy cream

1 tablespoon light rum

1 teaspoon almond extract

2 teaspoons baking soda

½ teaspoon salt

½ cup unsalted butter, at room
    temperature

1 cup superfine sugar

2 cups sifted cake flour

Chocolate Frosting (recipe follows)

*T*his is about the best chocolate cake you'll ever eat. A classic, old-fashioned dessert that says, "This girl really knows how to bake!" This is a splurge for those on restricted diets, but even the tiniest piece will satisfy your sweet tooth.

MAKES ONE 9-INCH
LAYER CAKE

PERFECT CHOCOLATE CAKE

1. Preheat the oven to 300°F.

2. Lightly butter two 9-inch round cake pans. Set aside.

3. Combine one of the egg yolks with the milk in the top half of a double boiler, whisking to blend. Add the brown sugar, chocolate, and allspice.

4. Place the top half of the double boiler over the bottom half filled with boiling water. Place over medium-high heat and cook, beating the mixture constantly, for about 7 minutes or until the chocolate has melted and the pudding has thickened.

5. Remove from the heat and lift the top half from the bottom. Set the pudding aside to cool.

6. Combine the heavy cream with 3 tablespoons of cool water and the rum and almond extract in a small mixing bowl. Set aside.

7. When the chocolate pudding has cooled, beat in the baking soda and salt.

8. Place the butter in the bowl of a standing electric mixer fitted with the paddle attachment. Beat for about 2 minutes or until light and fluffy, and then gradually beat in the superfine sugar. When well-blended, add the remaining 2 egg yolks, one at a time, beating well after each addition to incorporate.

9. Add the flour, alternately with the heavy cream mixture, beating after each addition to incorporate.

10. Add the reserved cooled chocolate mixture and beat for about 3 minutes or until the batter is very smooth.

11. To whip the egg whites, either use a handheld electric mixer or transfer the cake batter to another bowl and wash and dry the bowl of the standing electric mixer. Fit the mixer with the whip attachment and beat the egg whites for about 3 minutes or until soft peaks form.

12. Fold the beaten egg whites into the cake batter.

13. Divide the batter equally between the two prepared cake pans.

14. Place in the preheated oven and bake for 15 minutes. Rotate the cake and bake for another 10 minutes or until a cake tester (or toothpick) inserted into the center comes out clean.

(continued)

15. Remove from the oven and carefully invert onto wire racks to cool.

16. When cool, frost with Chocolate Frosting.

CHOCOLATE FROSTING

One 6-ounce package semi-sweet
   chocolate bits

¾ cup unsalted butter

½ cup half-and-half

2 ½ cups sifted confectioners'
   sugar

1 teaspoon pure vanilla extract

1. Combine the chocolate with the butter and half-and-half in a heavy-bottomed saucepan over medium heat.

2. Cook, stirring constantly, for about 2 minutes or until the chocolate has melted and the mixture is completely blended.

3. Remove from the heat and beat in the sugar. When incorporated, beat in the vanilla.

4. Transfer to a bowl, cover with plastic film, and refrigerate until ready to use. Bring to room temperature and stir to soften before spreading.

This is a wonderful cake. It's somewhat different from the traditional, Southern coconut cake that has a lemon filling and lots of sweetened coconut covering the frosting. The addition of brown sugar makes the cake itself somewhat richer and the unsweetened coconut has a nice fresh taste against the sweet frosting.

MAKES ONE 9-INCH
LAYER CAKE

2½ cups all-purpose flour, sifted

1 teaspoon baking powder

1 teaspoon baking soda

5 large eggs, at room temperature, separated

½ cup unsalted butter, at room temperature

1 cup vegetable shortening, at room temperature

1 cup packed light brown sugar

1 cup granulated sugar

1 cup heavy cream, at room temperature

1 cup unsweetened coconut

½ cup finely chopped walnuts

½ cup finely chopped pecans

1 teaspoon pure vanilla extract

Coconut Cream Cheese Frosting (recipe follows)

¼ cup toasted unsweetened coconut

¼ cup chopped toasted pecans

¼ cup chopped walnuts, toasted

COCONUT CAKE

(continued)

1. Preheat the oven to 350°F.

2. Lightly butter two 9-inch round cake pans. Set aside.

3. Sift the flour, baking powder, and baking soda together. Set aside.

4. Place the egg whites in the bowl of a standing electric mixer fitted with the whip attachment. Beat for about 4 minutes or until stiff peaks form. Scrape the beaten whites from the bowl into another clean mixing bowl. Set aside.

5. Return the bowl to the mixer and replace the whip with the paddle attachment.

6. Combine the butter and vegetable shortening in the mixer bowl and begin beating on low to blend. Add the brown and granulated sugars and beat on medium for about 4 minutes or until light and fluffy.

7. Add the egg yolks, one at a time, beating well after each addition to incorporate.

8. Add the flour mixture, alternately with the heavy cream , beating after each addition to incorporate.

9. Remove the bowl from the mixer stand and stir in the coconut, walnuts, pecans, and vanilla.

10. When well-blended, gently fold in the reserved beaten egg whites, folding until just incorporated. Do not over-beat or the cakes will not rise properly.

11. Divide the batter equally between the two prepared cake pans.

12. Place in the preheated oven and bake for about 40 minutes or until a cake tester (or toothpick) inserted into the center comes out clean.

13. Remove from the oven and let stand for 10 minutes. Then, carefully invert onto wire racks to cool completely.

14. When cool, place one layer, bottom-side up on a cake plate. Using a spatula, coat the top with a generous layer of frosting. Place the remaining layer on top, bottom-side down. Continue to frost the sides and top of the cake, swirling the frosting into peaks over the top.

15. When the entire cake is frosted, sprinkle the top with toasted coconut and toasted pecans and walnuts.

COCONUT CREAM CHEESE FROSTING

One 8-ounce package cream cheese, at room temperature

½ cup unsalted butter, at room temperature

3 cups confectioners' sugar, sifted

1 teaspoon pure vanilla extract

1 cup unsweetened coconut

½ cup chopped pecans

1. Combine the cream cheese with the butter in the bowl of a standing electric mixer fitted with the paddle attachment. Beat for about 3 minutes or until very light and fluffy.

2. With the motor on low, gradually beat the sugar and vanilla into the cream cheese mixture. When all of the sugar has been added, if necessary add milk, a few drops at a time, to thin to spreading consistency.

3. Remove the bowl from the mixer stand and stir in the coconut and pecans, beating to incorporate.

4. If not using immediately, cover with plastic film and set aside at room temperature for no more than an hour. For longer storage, refrigerate, but bring to room temperature before using.

3 cups sifted cake flour

½ teaspoon salt

¼ teaspoon baking powder

1 cup (2 sticks) unsalted
butter, at room
temperature

2½ cups sugar

6 large eggs, at room
temperature

1½ teaspoons pure vanilla
extract

1½ teaspoons orange extract

1 cup sour cream

½ cup apricot brandy

Confectioners' sugar for
dusting

*T*his is another simple cake that I've jazzed up a bit—this time with apricot brandy. But if you're not a lover of alcohol in desserts, just leave it out and increase the vanilla to 1 tablespoon. It's a great keeper—refrigerated, tightly wrapped, you'll still be eating a fresh-tasting cake a week down the line. And, if any is left, cut the cake into slices, give it a quick toast, a scoop of ice cream, and drizzle of chocolate sauce and you'll have a very special dessert!

MAKES ONE 10-INCH
BUNDT CAKE

APRICOT-BRANDY POUND CAKE

1. Preheat the oven to 325°F.

2. Lightly butter and flour a 10-inch bundt pan. Set aside.

3. Sift the flour, salt, and baking powder together. Set aside.

4. Place the butter in the bowl of a standing electric mixer fitted with the paddle attachment, beating to soften. Add the sugar and continue to beat on medium until light and fluffy.

5. Add the eggs, one at a time, beating well after each addition to incorporate.

6. Beat in the vanilla and orange extracts, beating to blend.

7. With the motor on low, gradually add the flour mixture, alternately with the sour cream and brandy, beating to incorporate.

8. Scrape the batter into the prepared pan and smooth the top with a spatula.

9. Place in the preheated oven and bake for 55 minutes or until a cake tester (or toothpick) inserted into the center comes out clean.

10. Remove from the oven and place on a wire rack to cool for 5 minutes. Then, run a knife around the interior edge of the pan to loosen the cake. Invert the cake onto the wire rack, lift off the pan, and let cool.

11. Transfer the cake to a serving plate. Place the confectioners' sugar in a fine mesh sieve and, tapping gently on the side of the sieve, lightly dust the top of the cake with sugar.

3 cups sifted all-purpose flour

1 teaspoon baking soda

½ teaspoon ground cloves

½ teaspoon ground nutmeg

½ teaspoon ground cinnamon

½ teaspoon ground ginger

1 cup unsalted butter, at room temperature

2 cups sugar

3 large eggs

1 cup buttermilk

1 cup blackberry jam

1 cup golden raisins

1 cup chopped pecans or walnuts

Confectioners' sugar for dusting

*T*his is a real old-fashioned kind of cake. It probably comes from a time when jam was made at home and spices were special, so it was only prepared for celebrations. In the South, cooks often add chopped candied fruit and then ice the cake with a rich cream cheese frosting.

MAKES ONE 10-INCH CAKE

BLACKBERRY JAM-SPICE CAKE

1. Preheat the oven to 350°F.

2. Lightly spray the interior of a 10-inch nonstick tube pan with nonstick vegetable spray.

3. Sift the flour, baking soda, cloves, nutmeg, cinnamon, and ginger together. Set aside.

4. Place the butter in the bowl of a standing electric mixer fitted with the paddle attachment. Beat on low to just soften. Add the sugar and beat for about 4 minutes or until light and fluffy.

5. Add the eggs and beat to incorporate.

6. Add the flour mixture alternately with the buttermilk. When well combined, remove the bowl from the mixer and fold in the jam, raisins, and nuts.

7. Scrape the batter into the prepared pan and place in the preheated oven. Bake for about 90 minutes or until a cake tester inserted into the center comes out clean.

8. Remove from the oven and invert the cake onto a wire rack. Remove the pan and allow the cake to cool.

9. Transfer the cake to a serving plate. Place the confectioners' sugar in a fine mesh sieve and, tapping gently on the side of the sieve, lightly dust the top of the cake with sugar.

2 cups finely chopped carrots

1¼ cups craisins (or raisins)

1 cup finely chopped tart apples

½ cup finely chopped fresh pineapple

1 cup thawed frozen apple juice concentrate

1 tablespoon pure vanilla extract

1 teaspoon freshly grated orange zest

2½ cups pastry flour

2 cups whole wheat pastry flour

½ cup sugar substitute

1 tablespoon baking powder

1 tablespoon ground cinnamon

1 teaspoon pumpkin pie spice

1 teaspoon baking soda

½ cup low-fat buttermilk

½ cup nonfat vanilla yogurt

1 cup chopped toasted pecans or walnuts, optional

3 large egg whites, beaten until stiff

*T*his cake got its name because I'm always telling people on a diet or with any kind of health issue, "You really can eat this cake!" The only sweetness comes from the sugar substitute, fruit and apple juice concentrate—and there are no egg yolks, either. I prefer it served warm with a scoop of frozen, nonfat vanilla yogurt or sugar-free vanilla ice cream.

MAKES ONE 10-INCH CAKE

YOU REALLY CAN EAT IT CARROT CAKE

1. Combine the carrots, craisins, apples, and pineapple, in a plastic container with a lid. Stir in the apple juice concentrate, vanilla, and orange zest. Cover and refrigerate for at least 3 hours or up to 12 hours.

2. Preheat the oven to 350°F.

3. Lightly coat the interior of a 10-inch tube cake pan with nonstick vegetable spray.

4. Combine the pastry flours with the sugar substitute, baking powder, cinnamon, pie spice, and baking soda in a large mixing bowl. Make a well in the center and pour in the marinated carrot mixture. Stir to just combine. Add the buttermilk and yogurt, beating to fully incorporate. Fold in the nuts, if using, and then the beaten egg whites.

5. Scrape the batter into the prepared pan and place in the preheated oven. Bake for about 1 hour or until a cake tester inserted near the center comes out clean.

6. Remove from the oven and invert the pan onto a wire cake rack. Remove the pan and allow the cake to cool.

2 cups all-purpose flour

1¾ cups sugar

2 teaspoons baking powder

½ teaspoon salt

2 large eggs, at room temperature

1½ cups heavy cream

1 quart strawberries, well-washed and patted dry

¾ cup blueberries

2 teaspoons pure vanilla extract

1 large banana, peeled and cut, crosswise, into thin slices

1 cup whipped cream

*T*his is similar to a strawberry shortcake, but I think it's even better than the old-fashioned biscuit variety. It's easy to make—just make sure you have enough cream on hand to dollop big puffs of whipped cream on top of the finished cake.

MAKES ONE 9-INCH X 13-INCH CAKE

CREAM CAKE WITH FRESH BERRIES AND BANANAS

1. Preheat the oven to 325°F.

2. Butter and flour a 9-inch × 11-inch baking dish. Set aside.

3. Combine the flour, 1½ cups of the sugar, baking powder, and salt in a large mixing bowl. Add the eggs and cream, beating with a wooden spoon to a smooth batter.

4. Scrape the batter into the prepared pan and place into the preheated oven. Bake for about 45 minutes or until a cake tester (or toothpick) inserted into the center comes out clean.

5. Remove from the oven and place on a wire rack to cool for at least 30 minutes before cutting.

6. While the cake is cooling, combine the strawberries and blueberries with the remaining ¼ cup sugar and vanilla, stirring to blend. Set aside to macerate for 20 minutes.

7. When ready to serve, fold the bananas into the berry mixture. Spoon the fruit with the juice over the cake. Top with dollops of whipped cream and serve.

1 cup dark corn syrup

1 cup light brown sugar

10 Jazz or Braeburn apples, peeled, cored, and sliced

1½ teaspoons ground cinnamon

1½ teaspoons ground nutmeg

1 teaspoon cornstarch

1 teaspoon freshly grated orange zest

1 teaspoon freshly grated lemon zest

2 tablespoons unsalted butter, at room temperature

One package refrigerated 2-crust piecrust

1 large egg

½ tablespoon milk

I love, love, love Jazz apples, which I get from specialty produce stores—but you can use any crisp, slightly tart apple to make this dessert. I call it "fried" simply because the apples are cooked on the stovetop in a frying pan. Let's just say it's my healthier version of a fried pie!

MAKES ONE 9-INCH PIE

FRIED APPLE PIE

1. Preheat the oven to 325°F.

2. Lightly coat a 9-inch glass pie plate with vegetable oil. Set aside.

3. Combine the corn syrup and ¾ cup of the brown sugar in a nonstick sauce-pan over medium heat. Cook, stirring constantly, until the sugar has melted into the syrup, taking care that the mixture does not burn.

4. Stir in the apples. When blended, add 1 teaspoon each of the cinnamon and nutmeg, cornstarch, orange and lemon zests and the salt, stirring constantly to incorporate the dry ingredients. Cook, stirring occasionally, for about 6 minutes or until bubbling. Stir in the butter and remove from the heat. Set aside to cool before filling the pastry.

5. Place one of the pastry circles into the oiled pie plate.

6. Combine the remaining ¼ cup of brown sugar with the remaining ½ teaspoon of cinnamon and nutmeg, stirring to blend. Set aside.

7. Using a slotted spoon transfer the cooled apple mixture to the pie plate, allowing the excess liquid to drain off before placing the apples into the pastry. Mound the apples in the center. The apples should generously fill the pastry.

8. Cover with the remaining pastry circle, pressing the edges together. Using your thumb and index finger, crimp the two pieces of pastry together to make a decorative edge.

9. Combine the egg and milk in a small mixing bowl, whisking with a fork to blend.

10. Using a pastry brush, lightly coat the top crust with the egg wash. Sprinkle the reserved brown sugar/spice mixture over the top of the pastry.

11. Place in the preheated oven and bake for about 35 minutes or until the crust is golden brown.

12. Remove from the oven and let cool for a few minutes before serving.

*3½ cups cooked navy beans,
    well-drained*

1 cup light brown sugar

1 cup unsalted butter, softened

2 tablespoons cornstarch

4 large eggs

One 13-ounce can evaporated milk

1 tablespoon lemon juice

1 tablespoon ground cinnamon

1 teaspoon ground nutmeg

*B*ean pie is an example of great cooks taking everyday fare and turning it into something sweet and delicious. The pie also makes a nice side dish—just be sure to use less sugar than otherwise called for in the recipe.

MAKES ONE 9-INCH PIE

BEAN PIE

1. Preheat the oven to 450°F.

2. Place the beans in the bowl of a food processor fitted with the metal blade and process to a smooth purée. Measure out 2½ cups. (Use any extra to thicken soups or gravies.)

3. Place the bean purée in the bowl of a standing electric mixer fitted with the paddle attachment. Add the sugar, butter, and cornstarch and beat until well-blended. Add the eggs and milk, beating to incorporate . Finally, add the lemon juice, cinnamon and nutmeg, and beat to blend.

4. Pour the mixture into the pie shell and place in the preheated oven. Bake for 10 minutes; then, lower the temperature to 350°F and bake for another 40 minutes or until the pastry is golden and the filling is set in the center.

5. Remove from the oven and set on a wire rack to cool for 15 minutes before cutting.

This is another quick dessert if you have a well-stocked pantry and fridge. The dumplings can be made with sweet or tart apples—as I've said, I do love Jazz apples, so I would especially recommend them—and the sugar can also be replaced with your favorite sugar substitute.

MAKES 6

¾ cup sugar

1 tablespoon ground cinnamon

½ cup raisins

¼ cup chopped nuts

¼ cup melted unsalted butter

One package refrigerated 2-crust prepared piecrust

6 small ripe pears

PEAR DUMPLINGS

1. Combine the sugar and cinnamon with the raisins and nuts. Stir in 2 tablespoons of the melted butter. Set aside.

2. Cut six 5- to 6-inch circles (or circles large enough to enclose the pears by about three-quarters) from the pastry.

3. Working from the flower end, carefully core each pear without going up to the stem. Trim off the stem end and peel about 1-inch of the skin off around the stem. Stuff the cavity with the sugar mixture and then place a pear in the center of each pastry circle. Pull the pastry up around the fruit, pleating it together to make a firm fit.

4. Brush the top of each pear with the remaining melted butter.

5. Place the pears in a baking dish in the preheated oven and bake for 10 minutes. Lower the temperature to 350°F and bake for an additional 30 minutes or until the pastry is golden brown and the pears are tender.

6. Remove from the oven and serve warm with heavy cream or vanilla yogurt.

¾ cup unsalted butter

2 cups dark brown sugar

7 large eggs

2½ cups milk

2 tablespoons pure vanilla
extract

One 1 pound loaf challah
or other slightly sweet
egg bread, torn into
small pieces

2 tablespoons cinnamon
sugar

As far as girlfriends go, Diane is up at the top of my list. This girl is fierce! This is her special, very rich bread pudding that I can only allow myself a small taste of from time to time. But it is mighty hard to resist because it's sooooo delicious—it's sweet and luxurious, with a butterscotch-like taste to it. It's even better served up warm with a scoop of ice cream—vanilla, coffee, butter pecan— you pick. What a way to end a great meal!

SERVES 6 TO 8

DIANE'S SPECIAL OCCASION BREAD PUDDING

1. Lightly coat the interior of an 11-inch by 7-inch × 2-inch baking dish with nonstick vegetable spray.

2. Place the butter in a medium saucepan over low heat. Stir in the sugar and cook, stirring, for about 5 minutes, or until the sugar has melted into the butter. Remove from the heat and set aside.

3. Whisk the eggs into the milk and vanilla in a large mixing bowl. When well-combined, add the bread and stir to combine. Drizzle the warm butter/sugar mixture over the soaked bread, swirling it around so that it is evenly incorporated. Pack the mixture into the prepared baking dish, pressing down slightly. Sprinkle the top with the cinnamon sugar, cover with plastic film, and refrigerate for at least 2 hours or up to 12 hours before baking.

4. When ready to bake, preheat the oven to 300° F.

5. Remove the pudding from the refrigerator. Unwrap and place in the preheated oven. Bake for 45 minutes or until the top is golden brown.

6. Remove from the oven and let stand for 10 minutes before serving.

If you feel the urge, you can make the meringue weeks in advance as long as you store it airtight. If any moisture gets to it, it will collapse and be chewy instead of light and crunchy, so be careful! This dessert can easily be made with a sugar replacement, such as Splenda. It makes a beautiful, special occasion presentation that looks far more complicated than it really is—which, in turn, makes the cook look pretty good, too!

SERVES 8 TO 10

6 large egg whites, at room temperature

2 cups superfine sugar

1 tablespoon white vinegar

1 teaspoon pure vanilla extract

⅛ teaspoon baking powder

⅛ teaspoon salt

3 cups raspberries or blueberries

1 cup heavy cream, whipped

Mint sprigs for garnish

MERINGUE RING WITH BERRIES

1. Place the egg whites in the bowl of a standing electric mixer fitted with the whip attachment. Beat on medium until frothy. Slowly add the sugar and beat until almost stiff. Add the vinegar, vanilla, baking powder, and salt and beat until stiff and glossy.

2. Mound the meringue in the center of a very clean, nonstick cookie sheet and spread it out with a spatula to a neat 9-inch circle. Place in the preheated oven and bake for 1 hour. Turn off the heat and allow the meringue to set in the oven until cool. Do not open the door.

3. Remove the meringue from the oven and place on a serving plate. Using a serrated knife, carefully cut about ½-inch off of the top. Cover with berries and top with whipped cream. Break the top piece of meringue into pieces and nestle the pieces into the cream. Refrigerate for 1 hour before serving.

4. When ready to serve, garnish with mint sprigs.

I always make some kind of fruit salad for large gatherings because so many people have dietary restrictions. A fruit salad allows everyone to have some dessert without any guilt attached. You can use any kind of fruit you like—alone or in as many combinations as you like.

SERVES A CROWD

6 strawberries, stemmed and quartered

One 15-ounce can mandarin orange segments, well-drained

1 navel orange, peeled and cut, crosswise, into thin slices

3 cups cubed seedless red watermelon

2 cups cubed honeydew

2 cups cubed cantaloupe

1 cup halved red seedless grapes

¼ cup unsweetened pineapple juice

1 tablespoon lemon juice

Mint sprigs for garnish

GOOD FOR YOU FRUIT SALAD

1. Combine the strawberries, mandarin segments, orange slices, watermelon, honeydew, cantaloupe, and grapes in a large serving bowl. Stir in the juices, cover, and refrigerate for 1 hour or until well-chilled.

2. Serve, garnished with mint sprigs.

LIST OF RECIPES

HOT 'N' SPICY (LIKE ME!)

Zuri's Hot Like That Buffalo Wings, 26
LaBelle Spiced-Up Beef Tips, 28
Sloppy Joes à la Patti, 29
My Favorite Spiced Beef Ribs, 30
Sassy Chicken Parmesan, 32
Mama's Ole Time Shrimp Creole, 34
LaBelle Seafood Salad, 36
Spicy Dirty Rice, 38
Miss Patti's Cabbage Shuffle, 40
Vidalia Onion Blossom, 42
Ooh-La-LaBelle Turkey Chili, 44
Miss Patti's Hot Cheese Biscuits, 46

DOWN-HOME STICK TO YOUR RIBS MEALS

White Bean and Collard Green Soup, 52
Soothe Your Soul Potato Soup, 54
Bangin' Brisket, 56
Short Ribs in Brown Gravy, 58
Smothered Pork Chops, 60
Baked Blackened Catfish, 62
Good Ole Gumbo, 64
Spicy Southern-Fried Turkey Wings, 66
Down-Home Fish and Chips, 68
Salmon and Grits by Norma, 70
Over the Top, Top, Top Macaroni and Cheese, 72
Perfectly Seasoned Mean Greens, 74
Fierce Fried Corn, 75
Fried Green Tomatoes, 76
Pickled Beets, 77

LIGHT & HEALTHY (BUT IT STILL TASTES GREAT!)

Light Vegetable Soup with Chicken, 82
Hot and Sassy Gazpacho, 84
Gentle Lentil, Chicken & Barley Soup, 85
Quick and Easy Pork Tenderloin, 87
Turkey Burgers, 89
Grilled Chicken Breasts with Pico de Gallo, 90
Jerk Seasoned Chicken and Pepper Sauté, 92
Broiled Snapper with Herbs, 94

Grilled Mixed Vegetables, 96
Sautéed Okra, Corn & Tomatoes, 98
Oven-Baked Fries, 99
Shrimp & Celery Salad, 100
Three Bean Salad, 101
As Good As It Gets Cornbread, 102
Watermelon Cooler, 103

SMACK YO' MAMA SEAFOOD

Mama's Fried Porgies, 108
Blackened Grilled Halibut, 109
Grilled Tuna with Wasabi Hollandaise, 110
My House Tuna Melts, 112
Salmon with Lemon-Chile Butter, 113
Honey-Mustard Salmon, 115
Barbecued Salmon, 116
Salmon Burgers, 118
Deep Dish Crab Bake, 120
Sweet and Spicy Shrimp, 122
Baked Seafood Surprise, 124
Poached Salmon with Basil Cream Sauce and Fettuccine, 126
Simple Shrimp Linguine, 128
Tomatoes Stuffed with Shrimp Salad, 130
Shrimp Caesar Salad, 132

CELEBRATE! BANGIN' BARBECUES, BEAUTIFUL BRUNCHES AND HAPPY HOLIDAYS

Bangin' Barbecues

Just Like I Like It Fried Chicken, 138
Tender and Juicy Barbecued Baby Back Ribs, 140
Barbecued Shrimp, 142
Meaty Baked Beans, 143
Grilled Corn on the Cob with Chile-Butter, 144
My Famous Hot and Spicy Potato Salad, 146
Creamy and Nutty Cole Slaw, 148
Miss Patti's Pickles, 149
Lip Smackin' Pink Lemonade, 150
Sweet Tea with Lemon and Lime, 151

BEAUTIFUL BRUNCHES

Egg White and Cheese Omelet, 153
Hearty Breakfast Sandwiches, 155
Sweet and Savory Grilled Cheese Sandwich, 157
Spicy Cheese Strata, 158
Ham and Spinach Quiche, 160
Brown Sugar Baked Country Ham, 161
Herb Roasted Turkey Breast, 163
Sweet Potato Pancakes, 165
Homemade Sausage, 167
Sautéed Potatoes and Onions, 168
Chocolate Waffles with Berries and Yogurt, 169
Buttermilk-Pecan Bread, 171

HAPPY HOLIDAYS

Sweet Butternut Squash Soup, 174
Miss Patti's Leg of Lamb, 176
Tender-to-the-Bone Rib Roast, 178
Stuffed Cornish Game Hens, 179
Black-Eyed Peas and Rice, 181
Miss Patti's Favorite Lima Beans, 183

Corn Pudding, 185
Creamy Sautéed Spinach, 186
Creamy Garlic Mashed Potatoes, 187
Cranberry-Pineapple Relish, 189
Twice-Baked Sweet Potatoes, 190

CAKES, PIES AND OTHER
THINGS I SHOULDN'T EAT

Perfect Chocolate Cake, 196
Coconut Cake, 199
Apricot-Brandy Pound Cake, 202
Blackberry Jam-Spice Cake, 204
You Really Can Eat It Carrot Cake, 206
Cream Cake with Berries and Bananas, 208
Fried Apple Pie, 210
Bean Pie, 212
Pear Dumplings, 213
Diane's Special Occasion Bread Pudding, 214
Meringue Ring with Berries, 216
Good For You Fruit Salad, 218

INDEX

Almonds
    in Creamy and Nutty Cole Slaw, 148
Apple
    Fried Apple Pie, 210
    in You Really Can Eat It Carrot Cake, 206
Asparagus
    in Egg White and Cheese Omelet, 153
    in Grilled Mixed Vegetables, 96

Bacon. See also Turkey bacon
    in Smothered Pork Chops, 60
    in Soothe Your Soul Potato Soup, 54
    in Sweet and Savory Grilled Cheese
        Sandwich, 157
Beans
    Bean Pie, 212
    Meaty Baked Beans, 143
    Miss Patti's Favorite Lima Beans, 183

    in Ooh-La-LaBelle Turkey Chili, 44
    Three Bean Salad, 101
    White Bean and Collard Green Soup, 52
Bananas
    Cream Cake with Fresh Berries and Banana,
        208
Barbecue
    Barbecued Salmon, 116
    Barbecued Shrimp, 142
    My Favorite Spiced Beef Ribs, 30
    Tender and Juicy Barbecued Baby Back Ribs,
        140
Beef
    Bangin' Brisket, 56
    LaBelle Spiced-Up Beef Tips, 28
    in Meaty Baked Beans, 143
    My Favorite Spiced Beef Ribs, 30
    Short Ribs in Brown Gravy, 58

Biscuits
    in Hearty Breakfast Sandwiches, 155
    Miss Patti's Hot Cheese Biscuits, 46
Breads
    As Good As It Gets Cornbread, 102
    Buttermilk-Pecan Bread, 171
    in My House Tuna Melts, 112
    in Sloppy Joes a la Patti, 29
    Special Occasion Bread Pudding, Diane's, 214
    in Spicy Cheese Strata, 158
    in Sweet and Savory Grilled Cheese
        Sandwich, 157
Broccoli
    in Light Vegetable Soup with Chicken, 82

Cabbage
    in Creamy and Nutty Cole Slaw, 148
    Miss Patti's Cabbage Shuffle, 40
Cakes
    Apricot-Brandy Pound Cake, 202
    Blackberry Jam-Spice Cake, 204
    Coconut Cake, 199
    Cream Cake with Fresh Berries and Bananas,
        208
    Perfect Chocolate Cake, 196
    You Can Really Eat It Carrot Cake, 206
Cheese
    in Baked Seafood Surprise, 124
    Blue Cheese Dip, 27
    Coconut Cream Cheese Frosting, 201
    in Creamy Sautéed Spinach, 186
    Egg White and Cheese Omelet, 153
    in Ham and Spinach Quiche, 160
    in Hearty Breakfast Sandwiches, 155
    Miss Patti's Hot Cheese Biscuits, 46
    in My House Tuna Melts, 112
    in Ooh-La-LaBelle Turkey Chili, 44
    Over The Top, Top, Top Macaroni and
        Cheese, 72
    in Sassy Chicken Parmesan, 32
    in Shrimp Caesar Salad, 132
    Spicy Cheese Strata, 158
    Sweet and Savory Grilled Cheese Sandwich,
        157

    in White Bean and Collard Green Soup, 52
Chicken
    Gentle Lentil, Chicken and Barley Soup, 85
    Grilled Chicken Breasts with Pico de Gallo, 90
    Hot Like That Buffalo Wings, Zuri's, 26
    Jerk Seasoned Chicken and Pepper Sauté, 92
    Just Like I Like It Fried Chicken, 138
    Light Vegetable Soup with Chicken, 82
    Sassy Chicken Parmesan, 32
Chocolate
    Chocolate Frosting, 198
    Chocolate Waffles with Berries and Yogurt,
        169
    Perfect Chocolate Cake, 196
Collard greens
    Perfectly Seasoned Mean Greens, 74
    White Bean and Collard Green Soup, 52
Corn
    Corn Pudding, 185
    Fierce Fried Corn, 75
    Grilled Corn On The Cob with Chile-Butter,
        144
    in Miss Patti's Good Ole Gumbo, 64
    Sautéed Okra, Corn and Tomatoes, 98
Cornbread
    As Good As It Gets Cornbread, 102
Cornish hens
    Stuffed Cornish Game Hens, 179
Crab
    in Baked Seafood Surprise, 124
    Deep Dish Crab Bake, 120
    in LaBelle Seafood Salad, 36

Desserts
    Apricot-Brandy Pound Cake, 202
    Bean Pie, 212
    Blackberry Jam-Spice Cake, 204
    Coconut Cake, 199
    Cream Cake with Berries and Bananas, 208
    Fried Apple Pie, 210
    Good For You Fruit Salad, 218
    Meringue Ring with Berries, 216
    Pear Dumplings, 213
    Perfect Chocolate Cake, 196

Desserts (*cont.*)
~~Special Occasion Bread Pudding, Diane's, 214~~
You Really Can Eat It Carrot Cake, 206
Dips
Blue Cheese Dip, 27
Dressings
Caesar Dressing, 133
Dumplings
Pear Dumplings, 213

Eggs
Egg White and Cheese Omelet, 153
in Hearty Breakfast Sandwiches, 155
in My Famous Hot and Spicy Potato Salad, 146
in Shrimp Caesar Salad, 132

Fettuccine. *See* Pasta
Fish. *See also* Seafood
Baked Blackened Catfish, 62
Barbecued Salmon, 116
Blackened Grilled Halibut, 109
Broiled Salmon with Lemon-Chile Butter, 113
Broiled Snapper with Herbs, 94
Down Home Fish and Chips, 68
in Good Ole Gumbo, 64
Grilled Tuna with Wasabi Hollandaise, 110
Honey-Mustard Salmon, 115
Mama's Fried Porgies, 108
My House Tuna Melts, 112
Poached Salmon with Basil Cream Sauce and Fettuccine, 126
Fruit
Cream Cake with Fresh Berries and Bananas, 208
Fruit and Nut Stuffing, 180
Good For You Fruit Salad, 218
Pear Dumplings, 213

Garlic
Creamy Garlic Mashed Potatoes, 187
Gravy. *See also* Sauces
Short Ribs in Brown Gravy, 58
Smothered Pork Chops, 60

Greens. *See* Collard greens

Ham
in Black-Eyed Peas and Rice, 181
Brown Sugar Baked Country Ham, 161
Ham and Spinach Quiche, 160
Honey-Mustard
Honey-Mustard Salmon, 115

Lamb
Miss Patti's Leg of Lamb, 176
Lemon
Broiled Salmon with Lemon-Chile Butter, 113
Lip Smackin' Pink Lemonade, 150
Sweet Tea with Lemon and Lime, 151
Lime
Sweet Tea with Lemon and Lime, 151
Linguine. *See* Pasta
Lobster
in Over the Top, Top, Top Macaroni and Cheese, 72

Meat dishes. *See also* Beef; Ham; Chicken; Cornish hens; Turkey
Bangin' Brisket, 56
in Black-Eyed Peas and Rice, 181
Brown Sugar Baked Country Ham, 161
Ham and Spinach Quiche, 160
LaBelle Spiced-Up Beef Tips, 28
in Meaty Baked Beans, 143
Miss Patti's Leg of Lamb, 176
My Favorite Spiced Beef Ribs, 30
Quick and Easy Pork Tenderloin, 87
Short Ribs in Brown Gravy, 58
Smothered Pork Chops, 60
Tender and Juicy Barbecued Baby Back Ribs, 140
Tender-to-the-Bone Rib Roast, 178
Mushrooms
in Grilled Mixed Vegetables

Nuts
Buttermilk-Pecan Bread, 171
Creamy and Nutty Cole Slaw, 148

Onions
   Sautéed Potatoes and Onions, 168
   Vidalia Onion Blossom, 42

Pasta
   Poached Salmon with Basil Cream Sauce and
      Fettuccine, 126
   Simple Shrimp Linguine, 128
Peppers
   Jerk Seasoned Chicken and Pepper Sauté, 92
Pies
   Bean Pie, 212
   Fried Apple Pie, 210
Pineapple
   Cranberry-Pineapple Relish, 189
Porgies. See Fish
Pork
   in Black-Eyed Peas and Rice, 181
   Brown Sugar Baked Country Ham, 161
   in Good Ole Gumbo, 64
   Ham and Spinach Quiche, 160
   Short Ribs in Brown Gravy, 58
   Tender and Juicy Barbecued Baby Back Ribs,
      140
   Tender-to-the-Bone Rib Roast, 178
Potatoes
   Creamy Garlic Mashed Potatoes, 187
   My Famous Hot and Spicy Potato Salad, 146
   Sautéed Potatoes and Onions, 168
   Soothe Your Soul Potato Soup, 54
   Sweet Potato Pancakes, 165
   Twice-Baked Sweet Potatoes, 190
Poultry. See Chicken; Cornish hens; Turkey
Puddings
   Corn Pudding, 185
   Special Occasion Bread Pudding, Diane's,
      214

Ribs
   My Favorite Spiced Beef Ribs, 30
   Short Ribs in Brown Gravy, 58
   Tender and Juicy Barbecued Baby Back Ribs,
      140
   Tender-to-the-Bone Rib Roast, 178

Rice
   Black-Eyed Peas and Rice, 181
   Spicy Dirty Rice, 38

Salads
   Good For You Fruit Salad, 218
   LaBelle Seafood Salad, 36
   My Famous Hot and Spicy Potato Salad, 146
   Shrimp Caesar Salad, 132
   Shrimp & Celery Salad, 100
   Three Bean Salad, 101
   Tomatoes Stuffed with Shrimp Salad, 130
Salmon
   Barbecued Salmon, 116
   Honey-Mustard Salmon, 115
   Salmon and Grits by Norma, 70
   Salmon Burgers, 118
   Salmon with Lemon-Chile Butter, 113
   Poached Salmon with Basil Cream Sauce and
      Fettuccine, 126
Sandwiches
   Hearty Breakfast Sandwiches, 155
   Sweet and Savory Grilled Cheese Sandwich,
      157
Sauces
   Poached Salmon with Basil Cream Sauce and
      Fettuccine, 126
Sausage. See also Turkey sausage
   Homemade Sausage, 167
Scallops
   in Baked Seafood Surprise, 124
Seafood. See also Fish
   Baked Seafood Surprise, 124
   Barbecued Shrimp, 142
   Deep Dish Crab Bake, 120
   Good Ole Gumbo, 64
   LaBelle Seafood Salad, 36
   Mama's Ole Time Shrimp Creole, 34
   in Over the Top, Top, Top Macaroni and
      Cheese, 72
   Shrimp Caesar Salad, 132
   Shrimp & Celery Salad, 100
   Simple Shrimp Linguine, 128
   Sweet and Spicy Shrimp, 122

Seafood (*cont.*)
~~Tomatoes Stuffed with Shrimp Salad, 130~~
Shrimp
  Baked Seafood Surprise, 124
  Barbecued Shrimp, 142
  Good Ole Gumbo, 64
  LaBelle Seafood Salad, 36
  Mama's Ole Time Shrimp Creole, 34
  in Over the Top, Top, Top Macaroni and
    Cheese, 72
  Shrimp Caesar Salad, 132
  Shrimp & Celery Salad, 100
  Simple Shrimp Linguine, 128
  Sweet and Spicy Shrimp, 122
  Tomatoes Stuffed with Shrimp Salad, 130
Side dishes
  As Good As It Gets Cornbread, 102
  Black-Eyed Peas and Rice, 181
  Buttermilk-Pecan Bread, 171
  Corn Pudding, 185
  Cranberry-Pineapple Relish, 189
  Creamy and Nutty Cole Slaw, 148
  Creamy Garlic Mashed Potatoes, 187
  Creamy Sautéed Spinach, 186
  Fierce Fried Corn, 75
  Fried Green Tomatoes, 76
  Grilled Corn on the Cob with Chile-Butter, 144
  Grilled Mixed Vegetables, 96
  Meaty Baked Beans, 143
  Miss Patti's Favorite Lima Beans, 183
  Miss Patti's Pickles, 149
  My Famous Hot and Spicy Potato Salad, 146
  Oven-Baked Fries, 99
  Perfectly Seasoned Mean Greens, 74
  Pickled Beets, 77
  Sautéed Okra, Corn & Tomatoes, 98
  Sautéed Potatoes and Onions, 168
  Twice-Baked Sweet Potatoes, 190
Soups and stews
  Gentle Lentil, Chicken & Barley Soup, 85
  Hot and Sassy Gazpacho, 84

Light Vegetable Soup with Chicken, 82
~~Soothe Your Soul Potato Soup, 54~~
Sweet Butternut Squash Soup, 174
White Bean and Collard Green Soup, 52
Spinach
  Creamy Sautéed Spinach, 186
  Ham and Spinach Quiche, 160
Squash
  Sweet Butternut Squash Soup, 174
Stews. *See* Soups and stews
Sweet potatoes. *See* Potatoes

Tomatoes
  Fried Green Tomatoes, 76
  Sautéed Okra, Corn & Tomatoes, 98
  Tomatoes Stuffed with Shrimp Salad, 130
Tuna
  Grilled Tuna with Wasabi Hollandaise, 110
  My House Tuna Melts, 112
Turkey
  Herb-Roasted Turkey Breast, 163
  in Homemade Sausage, 167
  in Miss Patti's Favorite Lima Beans, 183
  Ooh-La-LaBelle Turkey Chili, 44
  in Perfectly Seasoned Mean Greens, 74
  in Sloppy Joes a la Patti, 29
  in Spicy Dirty Rice, 38
  Spicy Southern-Fried Turkey Wings, 66
  Turkey Burgers, 89
Turkey bacon
  in Smothered Pork Chops, 60
  in Soothe Your Soul Potato Soup, 54
Turkey sausage
  in Hearty Breakfast Sandwiches, 155
  in Spicy Dirty Rice, 38

Vegetable dishes. *See* Side dishes

Waffles
  Chocolate Waffles with Berries and Yogurt,
    169